FÊTE

JUNG LEE
WITH KATHLEEN BOYES

FÊTE
THE WEDDING
EXPERIENCE

Stewart, Tabori & Chang • New York

Published in 2007 by Stewart, Tabori & Chang
An imprint of Harry N. Abrams, Inc.

Text copyright © 2007 by Jung Lee

Credits appear on page 239.

Library of Congress Cataloging-in-Publication Data

Lee, Jung, 1972-The fete wedding experience / Jung Lee. p. cm.
ISBN-13: 978-1-58479-628-2 1. Weddings—United States—Planning.
2. Wedding etiquette—United States. I. Title.

HQ745.L42
2007395.2'2—dc22
2007022868

Editor: Jennifer Levesque
Designer: Yaël Eisele
Production Manager: Jacquie Poirier

The text of this book was composed in Berthold Akzidenz Grotesque,
Bickham Script Pro, Bodoni Twelve, and Didot.

Printed and bound in China

10 9 8 7 6 5 4 3 2 1

HNA ▣▢▢▢▢
harry n. abrams, inc.
a subsidiary of La Martinière Groupe

115 West 18th Street
New York, NY 10011
www.hnabooks.com

To my beloved husband and partner, Joshua Brooks.
Never in a million years did I think I would be a
wedding planner, but then again, never in a million
years did I think I could be so happily married.
Without you, I could not do what I do. You are the
unsung hero at Fête. Thank you for giving me
the encouragement, strength, freedom, and patience
every day for my creative process. This book,
and our business, would not be possible without you.

CONTENTS

ACKNOWLEDGMENTS

This book and the success of my career are made possible by the many wonderful and generous individuals I've encountered over the years, and I would like to take this special opportunity to name them.

First, thank you to all of our clients who have allowed us to help create and design their weddings. It is truly an honor and privilege to have been a part of those most intimate and personal celebrations. I treasured getting to know each and every one of you during the planning process. Without your faith and trust in me, I could not have developed my talent. And a special thank you to those clients who granted us permission to feature their personal wedding photographs and stories in this book.

We are so fortunate to be able to work with some of the best photographers in the country. This book would not have been possible without the beautiful, artful photographs by Philippe Cheng, Shawn Connell at Christian Oth Studios, and Jeremy Saladyga at Gruber Photographers. A special acknowledgment to the amazingly talented Christian Oth. Thank you for being so incredibly generous with your valuable time. When I wanted to reshoot, you just fit me into your busy schedule and made it happen, and all with a smile.

I have had the incredible fortune of working with the top florists in the country. They understand weddings today are about so much more than just centerpieces; they work with the client to design and create beautiful one-of-a-kind weddings. They have taught me so much over the years, and I am so grateful to them. In this book, you will see stunning works by Ariella Chezar, Priscilla Schaefer at Glorimundi, and Lewis Miller from LMD Floral Events Interiors. I have learned so many things from Priscilla, who is the consummate professional and a joy to work with. It is obvious you are a true florist and gardener because your flowers are always so spectacular. A special thank-you to my friend Lewis. You are an extraordinary talent—I think I told you this the first time we worked together. I have learned so much from working with you, and I am a great admirer of you.

I am wild about paper products—the save-the-dates (in some cases weekends), wedding invitations, menu cards, programs…all of it. Thank you to Sloane Madureira at Russell Sloane for working with us on so many of our projects. You have a wonderful keen eye for fine design. Thank you to our talented calligraphers, who always help me out when I am in a mad rush: Deborah Delaney, Marian Rodenhizer at Castle Graphics, and Michael Sull at The Lettering Design Group.

I really have the best publicists. Thank you Marcy Engelman and Dana Gidney from Engelman and Co. I respect you immensely. You have always steered me in the right direction, taken care of me, and given me great advice.

Thank you to my literary agent, Adam Chromy, at Artists and Artisans. I appreciate how you always cut to the chase. Thank you for believing in me and always looking out for my interest. I also want to thank my former client Melanie Milgram for introducing me to Adam. You said to talk to Adam because he is good. And you were right!

A special, heartfelt thank you to my brilliant co-writer, Kathleen Boyes. I felt connected to you from our first meeting and it only grew exponentially. You got me right away, and you kept me on track. You backed me up and made me feel sane when I thought I was going insane. One of my favorite parts of this book project is that I got to know you. You have influenced me more than you know. You are a gem!

I thank Yaël Eisele, our talented book designer. Thank you for seeing my vision through and truly caring about the details as much as I do. This book is a collaboration of our styles. You have been so terrific! Thank you to my editor, Jennifer Levesque at Stewart, Tabori & Chang. Thank you for being patient with me and allowing me to make this book the way I wanted it. This means the world to me, so I thank you from the bottom of my heart.

A huge thank you to my fabulous and incredibly smart staff at Fête. The success of Fête is largely due to all of your hard work and dedication, and I am forever grateful and indebted to you all.

Thank you to Catherine Guialdo, our senior floral designer at Fête. Your hard work, commitment, and dedication are much appreciated. I am always adding, changing, and modifying design, and you are always there with me, never complaining. You understand my vision for each of these ever so diverse projects, and it is so nice to connect; at this point words aren't even exchanged—you just know what I want.

I thank Greg Dravta at Aion Entertainment, a fantastic lighting company, for working with me over the years. You have been so kind and generous to me and my clients. I know I can always count on you despite the difficult and challenging requests I frequently throw your way.

At the last minute, I had a vision for the cover, and without the help of these individuals jumping on board immediately, it may not have happened. I am forever grateful to the following people: Christian Oth and his wonderful staff for capturing my vision; Mark Ingram, who allowed me free access to his magnificent bridal gown collection; Lis Pearson at The New York Public Library; John Olavarria, who came to the shoot after working God-knows-how-many hours, for hair and make-up; the wonderful Jessica Austerlitz from Fête for getting us the model; our beautiful model Allison Villapiano; and Mari O'Conner for fitting the model.

Finally, my deepest love, gratitude, and appreciation to my family and friends. A special thank-you to my parents who have instilled in my brothers and I that anything and everything is possible with hard work. My parents came to this country with their three small children. They barely spoke a word of English, didn't have jobs, or any kind of support system. They led exemplary, selfless lives so that my brothers and I could realize our own hopes and dreams. We will be eternally grateful for all they have given us. My mother, my heroine, always made me believe I could do anything. Thank you for this amazing gift. Thank you to my mother-in-law who is so loving and kind, always trying to make life easier and better for me. My work is demanding and commands a lot of my personal time, especially on weekends—she is always there to help. My husband and I, along with our son and daughter, are so blessed to have the wonderful, loving family and friends who surround us.

THE FÊTE PHILOSOPHY

INTRO

CONGRATULATIONS—YOU'RE GETTING MARRIED! THE JOY, THE EXCITEMENT... AND, YES, THE OVERWHELMING COMPLEXITY OF PULLING IT ALL TOGETHER.

Where do you begin? Even if you know next to nothing about planning a wedding, you want yours to be simply spectacular. Well, you're holding the right book. I live, breathe, eat, and sleep weddings, and I am here to show you how to create and produce an amazing wedding of your own.

My name is Jung Lee, and I'm an owner of Fête, a New York wedding planning company. We're not like other planners, and this is not like other wedding books. I'm not going to give you a checklist of precious details such as designing wedding favors or picking the right color palette for your bridesmaids' dresses—you don't need me for that. You also don't need me to dazzle you with corny sentiments that have nothing to do with who you are and how you live. What you need is for me to share the secrets behind what makes a truly unforgettable wedding.

The kind of information I'm talking about just isn't out there, and believe me, I've read every book on the subject. The industry is consumed with either unattainable fantasy images or, worse, peripheral, one-size-fits-all planning techniques. You're far smarter and far more special than that.

SO WHAT MAKES ME DIFFERENT THAN THE REST? I HAVE A FRESH WAY OF LOOKING AT WEDDINGS. I RESPECT TRADITION, BUT I INSIST THAT IT HAVE MEANING FOR THE PRESENT. WITHOUT MEANING, YOU'RE JUST GOING THROUGH THE PACES—AND WHAT'S THE POINT?

What you need is the passion I bring to my work every day. This book will serve as your surrogate planner. By reading it, you become my client, and I make you the same promise I make all my clients: follow my advice and you will absolutely love your wedding.

We've had people say, "If I pick great vendors, why do I need a planner?" The question presupposes that picking vendors is the same thing as planning a wedding. It is not! Just because you have the best caterer, the best band, and the best florist, your wedding may not be the best it can be (though these go a very long way). It's like cooking; having wonderful ingredients doesn't mean you're going to have a great meal. It's what a chef does with them that makes it great. A talented chef can make magic with even mediocre elements. Extraordinary weddings have a vision behind them. They reflect the couple through every element, and the key ingredient is knowing how to masterfully orchestrate it. That's where an experienced planner comes in. With this book, I will teach you to think and act like your own planner and bring your wedding together with a vision that could only come from you.

I am on a site-visit at Nevis. There are always so many possibilities as to how a wedding can flow. It is imperative for me that I am by myself for a few hours and see how the different scenarios will look and play out.

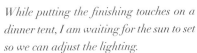

While putting the finishing touches on a dinner tent, I am waiting for the sun to set so we can adjust the lighting.

After building and operating a gourmet food store out of college, I decided to try building homes.

This is one of the last photos of me and my family in Korea before we left for America.

Here is a snapshot from my own wedding, before I had started planning weddings for others.

17

Critical as every element is,
planning your wedding
should never be reduced to
a checklist, with each
element given equal weight
and attention.

ONLY YOU KNOW YOUR PRIORITIES. BY FOCUSING ON WHAT MATTERS MOST, YOU CAN CREATE SOMETHING TRULY SPECIAL.

ONE OF THE MOST IMPORTANT THINGS I DO FOR MY CLIENTS IS TO HELP THEM PRIORITIZE WHERE THEY SHOULD PUT THEIR ATTENTION AND RESOURCES. ONE SIZE CANNOT FIT ALL.

Couples often blow a huge percentage of the budget on flowers. But do expensive arrangements really make or break the overall experience? You've been a guest at many a wedding. Is it the flowers you remember?

Like you, our clients are sophisticated and have great style. But sophisticated or not, it's easy to fall into the wedding trap of doing the predictable. Nothing makes me crazier than when someone thinks they have to do something "because that's how it's done." You don't have to jump on the conveyor belt. You have options—exercise them! If you've always dreamed about walking down the aisle to "Here Comes the Bride," then you should absolutely do it. But do it only because it has meaning for you. We've used modern songs from artists like Coldplay and Sting for ceremony music but performed them with classical musicians, using instruments such as guitar, violin, bass, and piano. The point is to question everything you think and everything you hear. Vendors often steer you in a certain direction because it's easier for them, not because it's right for you. You're unique and your wedding should be as well.

I did not set out to be a wedding planner, nor did I spend my childhood dreaming of being a bride. My passion was real estate, and I became a developer, working with architects and contractors to build retail stores and new homes. But like you, I met the love of my life and became en-

gaged. I wanted a great wedding and was convinced I could do it on my own. Why not? I thought. I have good taste, and I'm organized. I know how to pull things together. In addition to experiencing sticker shock at every turn, I quickly became overwhelmed with the details. I sought out a planner. It seemed there were only two kinds: the matronly, surrogate mother type, who had very established ideas about what to do; and the young, former-princess-bride type, who worked out of her apartment and wanted to re-create a version of her own fairy-tale wedding.

I couldn't relate to either. Neither offered the unique sophistication I wanted. I wound up planning my own wedding, and to be honest, I was very stressed, and that ultimately took away from the magic of the day. Afterward, I kept thinking I couldn't be the only one who experienced such frustration. There must be a better way. My husband Josh and I saw a business opportunity. Josh's background is in investment banking and operations, and we knew we wanted to work together. Fête was the perfect venture because I had a strong vision for making weddings so much more personal and interesting, while he could build a professional organization to support this vision. I could relate to my clients, and I wanted to take care of them and give them peace of mind so they could enjoy their day in their own style. Now I want to do that for you, too.

I'm committed to opening your mind to new possibilities, introducing different options, and guiding you through a process of introspection where you can figure out what you are about and then personalize your day. I want you to forget every cliché you've ever known and start anew.

I also want you to forget the word "no." Banish it from your vocabulary. Clients always give me a list of reasons why something can't or won't work. Too much money. Too inconvenient. Too pie-in-the-sky. Not enough time. The wedding venue won't allow it. I love a challenge, and I will push and push until I get some approximation of the fantasy. Sometimes it's as simple as asking. Other times it takes creativity. The point is, don't think in limitations—think in possibilities. This book is designed to be a source of great insight and inspiration while providing you with crucial advice along the way that will have a significant impact on your wedding.

Although I've worked on many elaborate weddings, I don't believe you need a big budget to achieve a sensational one. A little creativity goes a long way. Planning a wedding should be more fun than stress, more imagination than obligation. Our philosophy is to start with the fantasy and customize it into your reality. Unless you start with your dream, you can't possibly achieve greatness—and yes, you're aiming for greatness.

Ultimately, an incredible wedding rests on two things: personalization and orchestration of the entire experience.

Every element should be considered, every moment should be accounted for. Arriving at the ceremony with beautiful music playing. Romantic, flattering light. Timely service. Building energy throughout the event. Moving from one environment into another so there's a sense of flow. Little surprises at every turn. You want it to feel so special that no one wants to leave. Without question, your wedding is a production, and like all good productions, be it theater or music, success isn't about one element, but about all elements coming together with harmony and excitement.

To best illustrate our philosophy, I've organized this book by specific weddings we've developed. This way, you see the details in context, and I can better explain why we did what we did and hopefully inspire you in the process. Throughout, I will tell you what you absolutely need to know, what you can forget about, where you can cut costs, and where you can't. No matter where you live, I'll guide you on the big picture, and go over all the pertinent details, introducing new ideas and challenging many preconceived notions. (Unfan those napkins and don't even think about sitting at a sweetheart table.) I will tell you the stories behind these weddings, including what went right and, alas, what went wrong. (Yes, something unexpected always occurs, but its effect is in your attitude.)

My goal is to never let you lose sight of why you're doing this and what every part of it means now and in your future. At the end of the day, a wedding isn't just a fabulous party. A wedding is a union of two lives and two families. Every decision you make resonates, starting with the wording on your invitations. Your wedding is an experience that will be with you for the rest of your life. You are making your own history, and you will surely want to share it with your children and grandchildren, with everything that made it uniquely yours.

When it comes to your wedding, you get one shot to do it and do it well. And you can do it well. I'm here to show you how to have an extraordinary and personalized wedding with just a little imagination, an original touch, and some heartfelt planning.

NOW LET'S GET TO IT.

START WITH THE FANTASY IN MIND

1

You've slipped on the ring and called your family and friends. The excitement of your engagement is starting to be coupled with anxiety. Now everyone is asking you when you are getting married. You're getting stressed and starting to feel like you need to book a venue quickly in order to secure a great location. Not so fast. Believe me, I understand the temptation. Perhaps you're thinking that once you get the date and location out of the way, you can take your time with everything else, right? The problem with that is that by making the most important and hardest decision right away, you have started to paint yourself into a corner before you've even begun. I urge you to take a deep breath, step back, and let your imagination take over.

For the bride, Vail was a very special place. This is where she and her family had vacationed since she was a little girl. In spite of all the challenges that come with a destination wedding, this was the ultimate choice and a treat she wanted to share with her guests. What an incredible weekend it was indeed!

When I sit down with a couple for the first time, the location choice is far from my mind. Instead, I try to get to know the couple. How did they meet? What passions do they share? What places inspire them? How do they spend their leisure time? Are they foodies? Movie buffs? What makes them unique? I'll also ask them about their homes and their décor to get a sense of their style. Are they minimalists? Romantics? You can do this on your own as couple. How would you describe your styles and interests, individually and as a couple? Now ask yourself the most important question of all: if you had no constraints whatsoever, what would your dream wedding be like? Don't worry about budget, don't worry about your families or how many people you need to invite. Just describe your fantasy wedding aloud to one another. What would it look like? Where would it take place? What kind of food would you serve? What music would be playing? Don't hold back; like the root word suggests, fantasies are supposed to be fantastic.

This is not an idle exercise (although it happens to be fun). By exploring your wildest wedding fantasies, you get the creative juices flowing and can start to construct your own idea of what your wedding means to you. You may envision a highly sophisticated affair that takes everyone back to the days of 1930s supper clubs. Or perhaps you are all about a sleek, hip restaurant/club with a modern, cool, downtown feel. When it comes to details, you may find yourself focusing on the amazing food you'd serve. Or perhaps you'd have a live orchestra playing, or a great DJ, or both. Each fantasy can be an inspiration for the reality you're about to create.

THE STORY OF
Katie and Chris

Katie and Chris were not your average 20-something couple. They were college sweethearts who had lived together, and had a sure sense of who they were and what they wanted. I found them incredibly sophisticated and simply stated. They were also very visual, she being an art curator and he an architect. Katie and Chris were secure enough to want to do their own thing. I soon found out that Katie's passion was skiing. Her family had a home in Vail, Colorado, and some of her happiest times were skiing with her grandfather. She loved the winter wonderland of ski slopes and had introduced Chris to this world. Why not marry on a snow-covered mountain? As we talked about it, Katie and Chris kept saying they wanted it to be a sexy, hip, and ritzy affair. Knowing how difficult it would be to find accommodations at the height of the ski season, Katie's family thoughtfully secured a resort in the heart of Vail and made arrangements for 130 guests to stay in lodges and hotels for the long weekend. (Travel was a given in any event. Though Katie and Chris live in New York, she was originally from Las Vegas, while Chris was from Ohio.) Despite having the location, there were many challenges ahead, including the fact that the resort itself wasn't especially sexy or hip. Also, not everyone skis. So our challenge was this: to create a magical winter wedding during the busy ski season. One that would not require skiing—though that would always be an option—yet give guests the exhilarating experience of being atop a mountain blanketed in snow. Like all challenges, this one required a lot of creative solutions. I couldn't wait to jump in.

Through these illustrations, this save-the-weekend booklet shows Katie and Chris alone and later finding each other and falling in love.

SAVE THE DATE

Given the ski/snow theme, we wanted to give guests a hint of what was to come. Katie and Chris had a friend, an illustrator for *The New Yorker*, create the charming drawings (including the ones above) on the card shown here. Save-the-date cards are mostly functional. They notify your friends and relatives of your upcoming wedding date. Typically, they are mailed six months in advance. Anything earlier than that and they lose their purpose. (Do you know where you're going to be ten months from now?)

A FEW THOUGHTS TO CONSIDER

Save-the-date cards don't have to match your wedding invitation. You can be more serendipitous in style and paper. We'll show you a good example later in the book. These cards will matter most to your closest friends and relatives because they're the ones most likely to reschedule a vacation or turn down other invitations. You're free to change your mind. A piece of paper shouldn't dictate your wedding date if something causes you to change it.

As you can see, this was a winter wedding. I am a big fan of weddings in January and February.

1. Outside of ski country and warm-weather destinations, you can often find venues and vendors offering special off-season rates during the winter months.

2. Relative to the busy December holiday season, these months tend to be quiet. It gives everyone something to look forward to.

3. For the rest of your life, you'll have something to celebrate after the holidays.

4. Manage weather risk by recommending that important out-of-town guests fly in on Thursday. It is rare that airports are closed for three days straight.

INSIDER TIP
Timing is everything. Ideally, you should give yourself six to ten months to plan your wedding. You can accomplish most anything during that time. Anything beyond twelve months, in my opinion, risks losing momentum. Think of movies that are in development for years. By the time they're released, the vision gets lost.

Save the Weekend
January 18–21, 2007

Rooms will be provided for our guests
Details to follow

Denver International Airport
1 hour, 50 minutes by car

Vail
Colorado

Invitation to follow

MAKING A CEREMONY SPACE YOUR OWN

Very seldom do I accept a space as I find it. To me, everything is up for interpretation. The resort where Katie and Chris were to be married had a greenhouse which was just perfect for letting in the sky and snow all around us without actually being outside. But there were problems. First, it wasn't a symmetrical space, a pet peeve of mine. I also wanted it to look and feel different than it would if you were a hotel guest staying there. I looked at the space and realized that I could close off a wall of it and create a rectangular shape perfect for an aisle. My first idea was to make a wall out of white birch trees, which would have looked great. But the birch trees we ordered looked fake and the nursery couldn't pull up new ones because they were frozen into the ground. We then stripped the room of extraneous details, so nothing would distract from the nuptials at hand and the blue skies above.

HOUSES OF WORSHIP

Katie and Chris had a secular wedding. But what if you or your spouse-to-be are committed to a particular house of worship? You still don't have to accept it as is, especially if you find it dreary or dated. Add some inspired atmospherics. And I don't mean just flowers. Impossible, you say, your church/temple/mosque would never go for it. Perhaps, but why not ask before you assume no? As devoted parishioners, your family may have a lot of good will built up. Even if you're new to the congregation, ask anyway. I'm always amazed how if you simply ask for something with respect and the best of intentions, it can bring about the most positive outcomes. Here are a few ideas.

DIM THE LIGHTS
Lights direct attention. You may well want to highlight beautiful stained glass or divert people's eyes away from the walls in general by dimming the corners of the church.

LIGHT LOTS OF CANDLES
I find any space is transformed by an abundance of candles. I love white ones, but I also appreciate the mood that only red and amber colored votives can give. You can line the perimeter of the aisle or the room itself by bringing in tiered wrought iron stands for the votives.

LINE THE ALTAR AND AISLES
We've rented antique oriental rugs from a local rug store. They add lots of charm and warmth to the church, especially on a wintry day.

CALL IN A CHOIR
There's nothing more angelic than the sound of a children's choir. Once, we hired a boy's choir in full vestments and, when the children processed, had them hum "somewhere over the rainbow," a childhood favorite of the bride's.

HIRE AN OPERA SINGER
Second to children's voices, an opera singer is nothing short of spiritual.

SKIP THE FLOWERS
I only mention this as a point of interest, since traditionally you would assume that flowers would top the list of ceremony décor. Don't assume you need flowers, especially if you go for tiers of candles.

THE BRIDAL PARTY

THE ONLY RULE IS TO MAKE IT YOURS

As I said, Katie and Chris were open to new ideas, and that included their wedding party attire. Like most brides, Katie spent a lot of time shopping for a bridal gown. Nothing spoke to her. Finally, she gave up and decided to simply find a dress she loved. It happened to be a beautiful strapless silver lace tiered dress. She couldn't have looked more lovely or special, which is the whole point.

I urge you to forget any preconceived ideas about what a wedding party needs to be, much less look like. For example, the odds are very slim that a bride and her groom will have the exact same number of beloved friends and siblings. Don't force it. If one of you has six close friends and the other has three, so be it. An odd number is honest and real, and it's far better than calling in a so-so friend just to even things up. I have a friend whose mom was her matron of honor because they were truly best friends and there wasn't anyone she wanted more to stand up for her. Another bride called her "maid of honor" the "best lady" because she thought it suited the role better (I agree). You choose who walks down that aisle, including who you would like to give you away (your father, both parents, a sibling, or no one at all).

While we're on the bridal party subject, bridesmaids don't have to wear a uniform. Why would you want a friend to be uncomfortable in a dress she'd never pick out for herself? Color is a great way to visually unite bridesmaids if that's important to you. For my own wedding, I told my bridesmaids to all wear a black dress of their choosing, and they looked incredibly chic. Never feel locked into anything just because "that's how it's done." Remember, question every assumption and then do what suits you.

IF IT FEELS GOOD,
WHY NOT?

This small detail says a lot about Katie and Chris. While religion played no role in their ceremony, the official who conducted the ceremony suggested the guests call out "Mazel Tov!" the Jewish term for good luck that is also used in lieu of congratulations. Katie, in particular, thought it was a marvelous idea and a hearty round of "Mazel Tovs" concluded the ceremony.

The handsome groom and his grooms-men walking to the ceremony.

THE RECEPTION HALL
TRANSFORM THE ENVIRONMENT

LEFT: *The lounge area that connected the dining and dancing areas; during the dancing portion of the evening, guests could lounge here or go back to their table if they were not dancing.* RIGHT: *Guests conversing, dancing, and enjoying cocktails and bite-sized desserts.* FAR RIGHT: *Favors that Katie's grandmother purchased from a great New York chocolatier company.*

Katie's family had reserved the reception room of a five-star resort. I must admit, as wonderful as the hotel was, the reception space was not love at first sight for me. The ceilings were very low and the rooms were small with very little sense of flow. I sat alone in the space for a good couple of hours, and tried to focus on the space's possibilities, not its limitations. Here's what I came up with.

CREATE AN INVITING HUB

First impressions are everything, which is why I like to create a focus. In this case, we made the lounge area be the center of attention, almost like a foyer would be in a home. Everything led back to this area, giving guests a natural place to gravitate toward.

FOCUS ON THE TABLES

Rather than have people look at the room itself, we made the long tables the focus. I like 36-inch tables, which this resort didn't have. So we had plywood tops cut and placed on the 30-inch tables to widen them, which gave us room to create beautiful "tablescapes." This further kept the eyes on the tables.

DRAPE THE WALLS

When you don't like the walls, erase them—or at least drape them in a beautiful fabric. I like the gauziness of white sheers. You can back light them with color if you'd like.

BRING IN THE MIRRORS

This is one of my favorite tricks—mirrors, mirrors everywhere. While my original plan was to bring in ornately framed gilded mirrors on the walls, they proved unpractical. Instead of linens, we lined the tables with mirrors which served myriad purposes: first, they reflected the flowers and candelabras (and were a safe surface for the wax to drip on). Also, they gave the room a sexy sleekness it otherwise lacked.

ADD THE ILLUSION OF HEIGHT

There's nothing you can do about low ceilings, but there are things you can do to make them appear higher. Here we used lots of single candles and candelabras with tall (18 to 24 inches), thin tapered candles. The effect was elegant and lavish, with no one noticing the ceilings.

COLOR BY MOOD

Since Katie and Chris wanted a lush, decadent feeling for their reception, we went with the color of passion—red. We had floral arrangements that featured every red colored flower we could find, as well as pomegranates and grapes. We slipcovered the chairs in mix-and-match embroidered fabric and velvets for added texture.

ABOVE: *Before photo of the reception space.* RIGHT: *A rendering of our vision for this fantasy wedding.*

DECONSTRUCTING
THE LOOK

SILVER CANDELABRA WITH
TALL BLACK CANDLESTICKS

SILVER
CANDLESTICKS
IN GROUPINGS

COLLECTION OF
VOTIVES—AGED MERCURY
GLASS, ETCHED VOTIVES
IN JEWEL TONES

SILVER SCALLOPED-EDGED
CONTAINERS WITH BLACK
BERRIES

ALL THE TABLES HAD
CUSTOM MIRROR
TOPS, WHICH ADDED
INSTANT DRAMA

SILVER NAPKIN
RINGS—THE LADIES'
PLACE-SETTINGS
ALSO HAD FEATHERS

SOFT, SHEER IVORY DRAPING

TAILORED BLACK SILK
TABLECLOTHS

FOUR DIFFERENT CHAIR
COVERS—BROCADE, SILVER
BORDER TRIM, BLACK SILK
SOLID, AND VELVET

DIFFERENT WATER GOBLETS
ON ALL THE PLACE SETTINGS

SILVER URNS WITH MIXED
FLOWERS AND BERRIES

Guests getting into the snowcats to get to the mountaintop chalet for the rehearsal dinner.

Be sure to understand all costs you will incur (how overtime works, security, furniture removal, bartenders, station attendants, and so on).

Know your access to the space. What time can vendors load-in? Are any other events booked for that day? If so, find out when you can get access to the room for décor and when you have to load-out for subsequent events. Otherwise, you may find yourself having to cut off your party at the height of fun to set up for the next wedding.

Getting married in the summer? Find out how well the venue's air conditioning works. Temperature tends to shoot up when 175 people start dancing—can the air conditioning keep up?

Check out the bathrooms. Are they unpleasant? If so, make a mental note to dim the lights and use a scented candle to improve the atmosphere.

Are there any restrictions, such as having to use the venue's vendors? Know exactly what you're committing yourself to before agreeing to anything.

MAKING THE FANTASY REAL
FOCUS ON EVERY ELEMENT, NOT JUST DÉCOR

Décor is obviously an essential component of weddings, but great weddings are about the experience you and your guests have. It is the attention to detail within each area that makes the difference between an ordinary wedding and an extraordinary one. Katie and Chris wanted to give their guests a winter-wonderland experience. The beautiful environment went a long way on its own, but we added to it. The Friday night rehearsal dinner was held in a charming chalet-style club house atop the mountain. We had Vail ski lifts take the guests up the mountain, where they were greeted with warm apple cider before loading onto a snowcat that escorted them even higher up to the private lodge. To enhance the experience, we pumped in the James Bond theme music on the snowcats.

LEFT: *We asked for "the favor of a creative response..." for the response cards. The couple received all sorts of fun responses —poems, collages, drawings, riddles, old photos, and so on. We displayed them like a little art installation. Here, guests are seeing how other people responded.*
ABOVE: *Biscotti favors for guests to enjoy, homemade by Chris's mom.*

A FAMILY AFFAIR

It's the personal touches that keep the fantasy fun, as opposed to becoming a theme. Chris's mother is Colombian and for the Friday night dinner treated the wedding guests to her beloved Colombian-style chicken soup. She also baked her amazing biscotti as favors for everyone. Proving that thoughtful gifts need not be handmade, Katie's grandmother provided the wedding's favors—gourmet chocolates from the bride's favorite NYC chocolatier.

DESIGN YOUR OWN STORY

What if you don't have a fantasy wedding in mind? Does that mean you're doomed to an uninspired, cookie-cutter wedding? Absolutely not. Not everyone who gets engaged has a particular dream wedding in mind. In fact, most don't. The majority of our clients simply ask us to create a wonderful, memorable wedding without giving any more direction than the time of year they have in mind and how many guests they plan to invite. That doesn't mean we give them wedding model No. 53 from our portfolio. The goal is always to create a truly extraordinary wedding that is couple-specific. Remember, you are the hosts. More importantly, the wedding you create is the platform from which you begin telling the story of your marriage. This is your opportunity to create a personal environment that reflects you and transports your guests to a special world—one of your creation.

Instead of escort cards, we used the blackboard to direct the guests to their dining table. It was unexpected and fun! The handwriting really mimicked the bride's, so guests thought she had been working on it all night.

A CLEAN-SLATE APPROACH

Oftentimes, weddings have built-in restrictions of some sort: the family house of worship, a particular hometown, parents who are financing the wedding and want to have some input. Yet there are times when a couple has few, if any, constraints other than their budget. (Money is always its own constraint, even among the affluent.) Nowadays, bridal couples often plan and pay for part or all of their own wedding because they are older (she averages 27, he 29) and therefore often on their own. So let's say you're an established professional couple, both transplanted to a town or city of your choosing, and that's where you'd like to get married. You may not have family roots to draw from, but you have your own roots as individuals and as a couple. It is from those roots you draw inspiration. Your personality and passion set the tone and direction of your wedding. Again, what matters most to you? What do you enjoy? What do you most want to share with your guests? What kind of style, music, food do you love? You're planning the party of your dreams.

Here's another way to look at a clean-slate approach. Start with the end in mind and ask yourself what impression you'd like to leave with your guests when they think about your wedding. Do you want them to feel it was elegant and a chance to dress black-tie? Or would you prefer it to be more laid back and casual? Do you want them to have had a blast? Do you want them to remember the music and dancing? Or do you want them to feel like they've been to the best restaurant in the world? Focus on the feeling and then get into the specifics. You don't need a theme or a color scheme, just a genuine desire to make your day unique and your guests feel pampered.

JIM	2
CARI	7
DAVID	1
JENNIFER	
NANCY	
ADAM	1
nzie IAN	2
HALL ELLERY	3
rthy JEN	6
ARTY CLANCY	2
ARTY KIM	6
ARTY MICHAEL	6
LINTOCK AMANDA	6
Phee JAMIE	2
Phee MAGGIE	9
esta MANUEL	9
MEYERS BOB	6
MEYERS ELLIE	8
MILLER BENNETT	8
MOSHELAK DAVID	1
INEZ	1

POST	ANNE	
POST	MIKE	2
RAPPAPORT	MARCIA	9
RICHMAN	NANCY	9
RICHMAN	SANDY	9
ROBINSON	GALE	8
ROSARIO	PATRICK	6
RUDERMAN	ROSE	9
SALICK	ANNAMARTINE	1
SAPIANO	TONY	
SCHNUR	MIKE	
SCOLARO	PAUL	
SEARS	LISA	
SHANE	CHRISTINA	
SHANE	DAVID	
SHARE	MARK	
SHUMAN	MICHELE	
SILVER	ERIC	
SILVER	KATHLEEN	
SIMON	GENE	
	MARJI	
MON	MIKE	

THE STORY OF

Heather and Hank

Heather and Hank are the quintessential urban, professional couple. Both are independent, accomplished, and used to doing things in their own way. Heather is a graphic designer and owns a paper goods company, and Hank is the director of some of the most memorable commercials on television. They are incredibly charming, funny, and highly energetic; you can't help but adore time spent with them. Both were over 30, and it was a second marriage for Heather. Hank couldn't believe he had finally found and was marrying his dream girl. Serious as they were about each other and their marriage, they wanted their wedding to be a great party first and foremost. They didn't have a particular vision or fantasy in mind. But, they did have a wonderful sense of humor and a grand passion: gourmet food and wine. This was a couple that had their own wine cellar for goodness sake. They very much wanted to share their good taste (pun intended) and good spirits (pun also intended) with their friends and family. Our challenge was how to channel their passion for food, wine, and laughter into a night of love and entertainment for 160 guests. As challenges go, this was a great one. There were no set expectations, no preconceived ideas of what to do. Best of all, we had two creative individuals to inspire us and let our imaginations run free.

LOFTY FUN

For this wedding, we decided to go with a loft. Here's why: a loft would offer the most creativity. It would literally be a blank canvas on which to design a fabulous night, including ceremony, cocktails, dinner, and dancing. By using a loft, we could create the atmosphere, determine the room's flow and function, and guarantee the wedding would be entirely original in concept and execution. For these reasons, I love lofts and any other raw industrial space, such as photography studios and warehouses. Not only do they afford you the most creative flexibility, they are literally off the beaten path, usually located in a more remote part of town. You can also play your dance music fairly loud, as these spaces are rarely in residential neighborhoods. But I won't pretend they don't have their daunting challenges. I consider them high-risk, high-reward. You can minimize the risk factor substantially with intense planning and skilled professionals running and coordinating the wedding.

OPEN SPACES

Don't even consider renting a space like a loft, a museum, a government or office building lobby, or a warehouse unless you have checked the essentials on the next page. The goal of any plan is to minimize what could go wrong. (Since an open space is a blank slate, you are in charge of the set design, the direction, and the maintenance.)

A PROFESSIONAL CATERER

Honestly, when choosing a unique space for your wedding, this is where you pull out the stops. The caterer is the most important vendor, especially if you're not working with a planner. You need a caterer on whom you can rely to order and receive all the rentals—the appropriate tables and chairs; the proper linens, china, silverware, and serviceware; and the right staff—and we haven't even gotten to the food! Moreover, a great caterer will show you rental options, help you lay out the space, and schedule logistics, including vendor load-in and set-up. Remember, you are literally designing the space, which is why you need a professional to help you create a place to enter, hang coats, have cocktails, dine, and dance. This must all be worked out on paper and the caterer most likely will have the experience to know what works best and not to leave anything out. Many times, you have to double-duty the space (more on this later), so you need to work out with the caterer who is moving what behind the scenes.

A FLORAL DESIGNER

Rather than just thinking about the table centerpieces, this person should help you create the overall set design, including prop rentals, furniture lounge areas, suitable plants, and possibly draping. These design efforts should be coordinated with the lighting team. A floral designer is different from a florist.

SKILLED LIGHTING PROFESSIONALS

Lighting is key in an open-styled space. It sets the mood, defines areas, and helps create transitions throughout the evening, from cocktails to dinner to dancing. Most crucially, you need to have a lighting person or persons on hand all evening to adjust lighting levels as required. You may need them to refocus/change gels, or if you re-use a room, to re-program the lights. You also need to have professionals on hand if you have "intelligent" or moving lighting—the lighting that creates that "club" feel. Lastly, you'll need them to save the day if any electrical mishaps occur. The same holds true for your music vendor, be it musicians or a DJ. You want as few surprises as possible.

PLANS FOR GUESTS' ARRIVAL AND DEPARTURE

An important but often overlooked element of weddings is making guests feel special and taken care of when they arrive and depart. Simply put, they need to know where to go and how to get there. As the host and hostess, you need to eliminate any confusion with well-laid plans. Do your guests know where to park? Do they know where to enter the space? Once they enter, can they check their coats quickly, without waiting in line? When guests leave, is it safe and easy for them to find their cars? Is someone there to help them get a taxi or car service? Are there umbrellas for them if it is raining? These little details make guests feel welcome. Try to imagine the whole experience from a guest's perspective and don't leave anything to chance.

HOW TO REDUCE THE PRICE FOR THAT GREAT CATERER

OFFER JUST ONE ENTRÉE
A silent alternative, such as vegetarian platter or simple fish, should still be available.

ELIMINATE THE DESSERT COURSE
Serve your wedding cake instead.

SKIP THE FOOD STATIONS DURING COCKTAILS

LIMIT SELECTIONS TO LESS EXPENSIVE CHOICES
Chicken and fish are invariably cheaper than lamb or filet mignon. Salad is less expensive than an appetizer. If you make less expensive choices, make sure the caterer passes the savings on to you.

KEEP IT SIMPLE
Stick to an appetizer, the main course, and a dessert and skip a fourth course when offered. No one enjoys being stuffed anyway.

Not a single flower was used for this event. Chocolate brown tablecloths, natural ivory placemats, and perfectly arranged soy candles lined the dining table with touches of Hypericum berries and Bartlett pears. Ivory drum shades over the dining table completed the intimate look.

PENNY WISDOM

Do *not* skimp on quality vendors! I'm all for saving money and will show you many ways to do so, but if there's one thing I know for sure, it's this: your wedding is only as good as the people who pull it together. I'm talking about caterers, lighting professionals, musicians, photographers, videographers—anyone who plays a part in your day. This is not a dress rehearsal; it is your wedding. You have one shot to do it well. Forget family amateurs and that "friend of a friend" who will give you a good deal. Go with professionals who have true wedding experience. When things go wrong—and they will—you need a professional who will expertly know what to do on the spot.

When selecting vendors, you are much better off hiring a great vendor and scaling back the scope of their work than hiring the low-cost provider. There are caterers who will give you quantity at the expense of quality. It is much better to limit selection (no stations at cocktail hour and/or no choice of entrée at dinner) and go with the better caterer. I promise you, no one will go home hungry. The night should be about wonderful food and elegant service. At every turn, you want to opt for the vendor who has the highest standards for what they do.

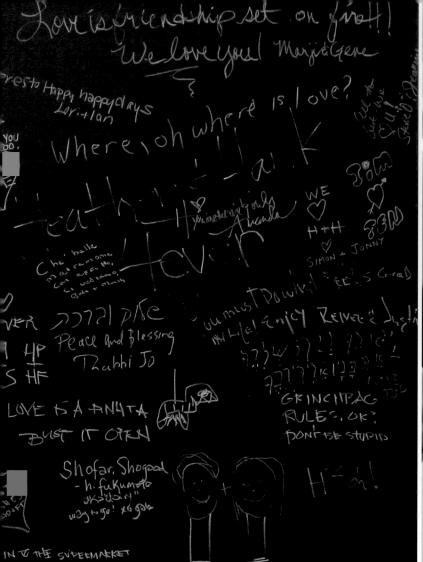

HANK FUKUMOTO

FAR LEFT: *We used two blackboards as a guest sign-in. We had a bowl full of fat chalk—guests doodled and wrote their well-wishes for Heather and Hank.*
LEFT: *For the place setting we used individual linen placemats, lined the glassware like a flight, used rounded-corner square plates as show plates, and added neatly folded napkins and menus on top. The guests' names were on the belly bands of the menus, which also served as seating cards. Here Heather decided to have some fun with Hank and gave him her last name.* RIGHT: *Portrait of the handsome couple.* FAR RIGHT: *In a clean, white loft space, we made a bar of fresh boxwood. We used white tumbled rock for the top surface, and flanked oversized nickel lanterns to frame the bar.*

The goal is always to create
a truly extraordinary wedding
that is couple-specific.

Cocktail setup: we hung one hundred maru paper lanterns, all in varying heights and sizes. The focal point was the spectacular, unexpected boxwood hedge bars. Two eight-foot-high black-boards were used for the guest seating assignment. Well-appointed topiaries completed this fresh, crisp look.

CREATING THE ENVIRONMENT

START WITH THE LAYOUT

Whether you choose a raw space or a traditional venue, you have to create a sense of place from the minute your guests enter the room. I consider the floor plan to be the most crucial element of design. It is the blueprint for the entire experience. The layout creates the mood and sets the stage for the flow of your wedding. Whatever the venue, you have the ability to tailor the room to your needs. You've seen the generic wedding setup a thousand times: round tables in a horseshoe around the dance floor. Wedding to wedding, the layout is often down pat. Get a floor plan of the space with clear dimensions. Now think about how you want to use the space and design it from there. Laying out a room can be simple or it can be complex. Each space has different constraints. Sometimes the room is too big, so you may fill it with an extra-large bar to make it more intimate like a restaurant or a beautifully furnished room. You may even opt to bring in a baby grand piano to fill in the space. Other times the room is too tight for your guest count and you need to get creative to make it feel comfortable.

This ceremony space was the definition of pure and simple. Two large urns were filled with magnolia branches, creating a focal point between them. Slipcovered benches and frosted beakers completed the look.

ONE ROOM, MANY MOODS

The loft we used for Heather and Hank's wedding was big, but not big enough to create single-use spaces for cocktails, the ceremony, dinner, dancing, and other activities. This called for improvisation. We kept the elements simple, and condensed furniture where and when possible. Colored lighting changed the atmosphere and mood. As guests moved from one activity to another, the staff was transforming the space they had just left. It was all timed to the minute. The loft was divided into two studio spaces. We chose to use Studio A for cocktails (which preceded the ceremony) and the ceremony because it made the most sense when it was laid out to have two distinct spaces within one large studio space. For the ceremony, some of the guests had to stand. But this was perfectly fine and, in fact, made the wedding ceremony even more intimate because the couple was truly surrounded by their guests as they said their vows. Immediately after the ceremony, guests were invited for dinner in Studio B. While they were dining we brought out large ottomans and pillows, reconfigured the benches from the ceremony to have a more "loungy" feel, and changed the lighting. All of these elements enhanced the atmosphere and mood of the ensuing dance party.

DRAPES
We used drapes to host cocktails and the ceremony in a single room. When the room was converted for dancing, the cocktail room became the dance area and the ceremony space became a smaller and quieter room for drinks and dessert (see adjacent photo). Drapes are the simplest and easiest way to create an intimate environment while screening out the rest. It's not supposed to be a wall; it's perfectly okay to see hints of what's going on behind the draping.

FABRIC-COVERED BENCHES
Slipcovered picnic benches provided the perfect ceremony seating. For the later part of the evening, custom pillows were used to cover the width of two benches, creating plush seating for the lounge.

A DEFINING BAR
Bars can edge the room or be the center of attraction. This one did both. We lined the bar in a freshly cut boxwood hedge to give the otherwise industrial room a dramatically fresh, unexpected touch.

PAPER LANTERNS
These are as beautiful and flexible as they are inexpensive and plentiful. Best of all, when you shine a colored light on lanterns, they take on a whole new personality.

PLANTS
Topiaries or other such trees or hedges add a focal point and soften the edges of a defined area. You can either buy or rent them, depending on where you live.

CHALKBOARDS
This was one of those necessity-is-the-mother-of-invention moments. There was no room for an escort table (the table that holds the seating cards). Inspired by Heather's handwriting, the guests' names and corresponding tables were written on the board. Blank boards gave guests a chance to write their good wishes. Later the boards were lacquered as keepsakes for Heather and Hank.

This is the same space that was used for the ceremony (see page 65). The two urns are still in the same place. As guests were in the other studio enjoying dinner, we transformed this space for the dessert and lounge. We reused the ceremony benches and put down over-sized seat cushions and throw pillows, which we lined up against the walls.

Bring the lighting up slightly when guests first enter the reception space so they can find their seats. Once everyone is settled, turn the lighting back down. As the evening progresses and music becomes more contemporary, I often like to bring the lighting down even more to further change the atmosphere.

FLATTER THEM WITH LIGHT

Be conscious of the sunset, especially during the summer. Not only do you want your guests to enjoy the sunset, you want to make sure to adjust the lights as the outdoor brightness changes the lighting in your cocktail and reception space. Before choosing a date and time, look up the sunset schedule.

Candles are the best, most inexpensive way to light a space and certainly one of the most romantic.

Consider using a mirrored ball—not in the center of the dance floor, but rather as a lighting effect. It gives the room a fun, energetic spirit. When done well, it is one of my personal favorites.

Small uplighting is inexpensive and makes a dramatic impact on a room or in a hallway.

THE RIGHT FOOT

When it comes to weddings, there are no rules other than those you invent to suit your purposes. Heather and Hank wanted to make sure everyone was in a good mood, so instead of starting with the ceremony, they started with a cocktail hour. Heather and Hank were there to greet everyone, she in a chic black cocktail dress. The fun part about this unorthodox approach was that it loosened everyone up and also kept them guessing as to what was next. That sense of unpredictability gave the whole evening a feeling of adventure and discovery.

MUSICAL NOTES

Music is a highly personal preference. There is no good or bad, right or wrong—only what you're passionate about. Heather and Hank were passionate about their music, and in their case, many different genres of music. We decided to go with a DJ. A great DJ is one who understands how to read the crowd and build energy throughout the evening. He or she doesn't want to be the MC or the center of attention. Using a DJ guaranteed that Heather and Hank would have the wide variety of songs and musical genres they wanted to hear; many were songs most bands couldn't play. Using a DJ also saved a lot of space in the room's layout. The music turned out to be a highlight of the ceremony. We coordinated Heather and Hank's procession so that the most poignant lyrics of their song coincided with their reaching the top of the aisle. This heightened the drama, anticipation, and emotion. Everybody felt it. A compilation of the wedding's music was made into a CD and given as favors to all the guests.

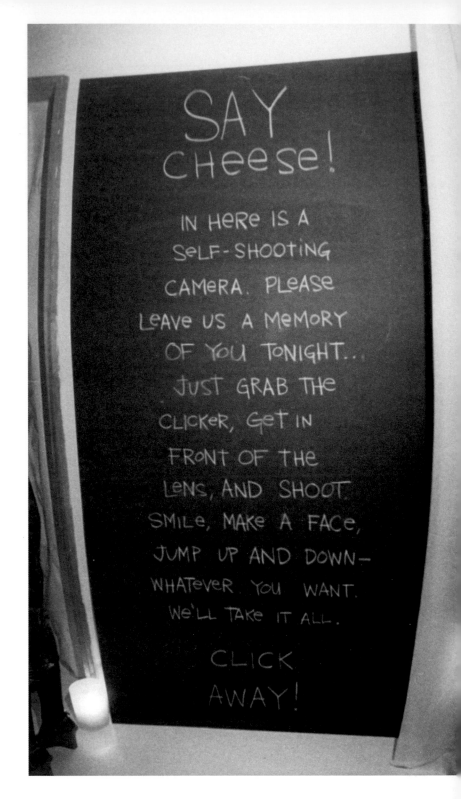

Heather and friends enjoying themselves in the photo studio.

Guests enjoying the menu — four courses, paired with wines in a clean, modern, yet intimate setting.

GREAT TASTE

Heather and Hank are major foodies, and their first idea was to hire a noted chef as the caterer for the wedding. As good as that sounds, it's a recipe for possible disaster. Catering is a very different skill from running a restaurant. Restaurants don't serve 160 people at the same time in a makeshift kitchen. Believe me, preparing that quantity and serving it all at once is an art form. I strongly urged them—and I urge you—against it. You can hire a chef to set a menu, but leave the execution to professional off-premise caterers who do this for a living. That's what we did. The chef designed an extraordinary four-course menu of Heather and Hank's favorite dishes: porcini tart, butternut squash ravioli, roast poussin stuffed with wild mushrooms, and rack of lamb in black truffle sauce. It was just what they wanted, right down to peanut butter icing on mini chocolate ice cream cones. Wine was served from their "stash" with a note that said waiters would only fill empty glasses since there were various vintages and vineyards. Heather's menu note said it all: "We're so happy to have you with us tonight. We love food, we love wine, and we love you!"

THAT PERSONAL TOUCH

To my mind, you can't have a successful wedding unless you include the kinds of touches that could only come from you. Here's just a sampling of the little things that made this a strictly Heather-and-Hank affair (or H+H, as the monogram read).

PERSONALLY WRITTEN PROGRAM NOTES
In her warm, quirky style, Heather wrote the program notes to the wedding, explaining their ceremonial choices. The booklet also included their childhood portraits, lyrics from Bob Dylan's "If Not For You," and a photo of their cat, Pawla.

A GOOD FRIEND INTRODUCED THEIR FIRST DANCE
Instead of having the DJ introduce them, Heather and Hank bestowed the honor on Hank's good friend Steve. The introduction was funny and heartfelt, giving greater meaning to the moment.

AN AWARDS CEREMONY
In the advertising business, Hank explained, we love to give out awards. So he had medals made up for prizes like "Best Guest" and "Best Mother."

SELF-DIRECTED PHOTO/VIDEO BOOTH
Rather than shove a microphone in someone's face while he or she is eating (a practice I despise), Hank let everyone leave a personal video in a MTV-confessional style booth.

A MATTER OF DÉCOR

WEDDING DÉCOR IS A VERY INTIMIDATING SUBJECT.

Most couples don't even realize that they have choices. You sign up with a venue and assume that's that: you get whatever tables, chairs, linens, and table settings they have. After all, isn't that what you're paying for? And won't the venue be aggravated if you come in and start redesigning the place? Is there even time to do such a thing? Worse than these fears, in my opinion, is thinking that décor is all about the floral centerpiece. That's like a woman thinking getting dressed is all about the shoes. Shoes may be important, but they alone will hardly get you out the door.

The modern approach to wedding décor is a holistic one. That means you take on the whole environment, not just a bunch of small elements. Everywhere you look, you have choices. My goal is to make you think about each and every one of them and not just go to the default position that the venue would prefer. You are the hosts. More important, this setting is the platform from which you begin telling your wedding story. The décor is your opportunity to create a personal environment that reflects you and transports your guests to a special world—one of your creation. Just as you want your home to look different from your neighbor's, you want your reception space to look and feel different from last night's wedding, as well as next Saturday's.

Just choosing different centerpieces will hardly make it feel different. Sometimes you only need to make simple changes to make a difference, other times you'll want to redo it all. There are no absolutes. Only you can decide where to compromise and what you absolutely must have. Because every wedding is unique, I can only offer guidelines from my experience, not hard-and-fast rules. You have to trust yourself and go with your gut. Believe me, you know what matters most.

THE STORY OF

Liz and Kevin

Some couples seem so right for each other that it's as if they've always been married. Such was the case with Liz and Kevin. College sweethearts, one is truly yin to the other's yang. Liz, a news journalist, is quiet and reserved, a woman used to listening rather than being the center of attention. Kevin, a trader who works at the New York Stock Exchange, is the more outgoing of the two, quick to smile and put everyone at ease. He clearly adores Liz and wanted to give her a beautiful and memorable wedding. Liz was not looking for a fantasy, Cinderella-style wedding. Even her gown was without frills; a strapless number with rows of ribbons, it was stunning in its simplicity. Similarly, Liz wanted a day that was beautiful and sophisticated, as well as welcoming to their 220 guests. The couple had chosen the venue, a grand and gorgeous ballroom known for its super-high ceilings and architectual details. The challenge here was a common one: to personalize a space that had its own strong personality and that many guests had likely already seen. The answer, we knew, lay in the décor.

THE ROOM AND THE TABLE
TWO ENVIRONMENTS, ONE MESSAGE

I am a firm believer in focusing your décor budget where you will be spending your time. For most weddings today, the majority of time is spent at the reception where dinner and dancing take place. At the reception, you have two important environments to work with—the overall room and the table—and two separate but unified impressions to make. This chapter is about organizing the environment, starting with the overall room. Why the room? It is the first impression your guests have, and therefore the most powerful. I promise you, the moment they walk in the room is the moment that sticks in their minds (which is why focusing solely on a single element like centerpieces is so misguided). Are you going for clean and modern, drama, fantasy, or a bit of all three? As we move into the décor process, you want to ask and answer that question for every component. As with designing a room in your home, an environment is created element by element. Do as much or as little as you would like, but at least know your options.

LEFT: *Even though it was a large wedding, the long dining tables made it feel very intimate.* MIDDLE: *Mini square escort cards with guests' names calligraphed in white.* RIGHT: *Individual menu cards with guests' names calligraphed on each card also act as place cards. Guests appreciate seeing the wonderful courses to come. Menu cards also allow guests with allergies or dietary restrictions to notify a waiter in advance of the arrival of a course.*

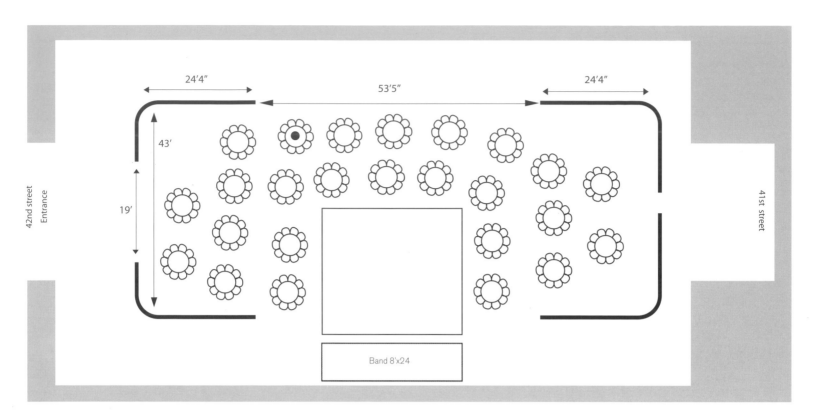

66" round

42nd street Entrance

41st street

24'4"   53'5"   24'4"

43'

19'

Band 8'x24

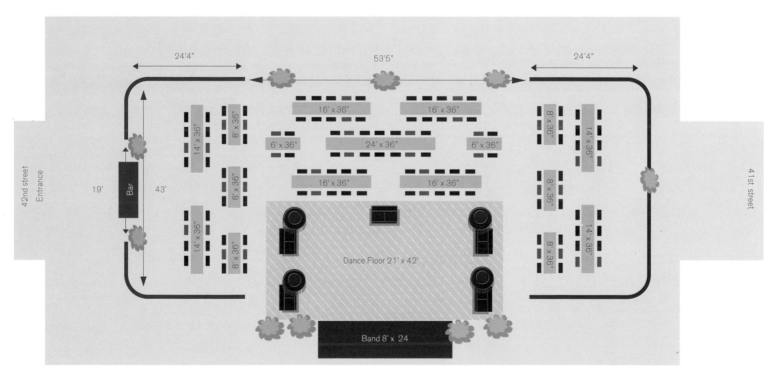

24'4"   53'5"   24'4"

42nd street Entrance

41st street

19'   43'

Bar

16' x 36"   16' x 36"

14' x 36"   8' x 36"   8' x 36"   14' x 36"

6' x 36"   24' x 36"   6' x 36"

8' x 36"   8' x 36"

16' x 36"   16' x 36"   8' x 36"   14' x 36"

14' x 36"   8' x 36"   8' x 36"   14' x 36"

Dance Floor 21' x 42'

Band 8' x 24

One of our goals is to make every guest want to stay until the very end so they feel like they didn't miss a thing. You foster that by having different places of interest and introducing new elements throughout the evening.

TOP: *A typical floor plan.*
ABOVE: *The floor plan we designed. Long dinner tables instantly make the space more intimate. Lush trees around the perimeter add life and warmth. Oversize lamp shades and ottomans define the dance area.*

IF THE ROOM IS BIG FOR YOUR GUEST COUNT

1. Create an oversized bar (with two returns, so it juts out and guests do not see the behind-the-bar clutter).

2. Enlarge/expand the dance floor 3 to 4 square feet per person.

3. Don't make the mistake of spreading the tables far apart. You want to keep the room feeling intimate.

4. Turn out lights on the periphery; if corners or sides are dark, they are de-emphasized.

5. Push the band more into the room, leaving some space behind them.

6. Create a lounge area in one corner of the room.

IF THE ROOM IS SMALL FOR YOUR GUEST COUNT

1. Consider dinner in one room and dancing in another.

2. If possible, put the bar just outside the room.

3. Go with smaller, narrower chairs, such as the 18-inch-wide Chiavari ballroom chairs. Large chairs can limit the number of guests at each table.

4. Using longer rectangular tables (36-inch width if available) will fit more guests into the room.

ASSESSING THE SPACE

In any venue, there are things you can change and things you cannot. Establish them in your mind right away. Size is first and foremost. The walls are a given and so is your number of guests. You have to reconcile the two, so that whatever the ratio, the atmosphere feels at once intimate and comfortable.

RULES OF THUMB

Here are some very rough calculations for space. Do not get hung up on the numbers. I offer this ratio just so you have an idea if you should be visually shrinking or expanding your layout.

COCKTAIL ROOM: 15 to 20 square feet for every guest.* Allow seating for 25 to 35 percent of your guests
DINNER AND DANCING ROOM: 20 to 30 square feet per guest
JUST DINNER: 15 to 20 square feet per guest
DESSERT AND DANCING: 20 to 25 square feet per guest**

This calculation allows for a bar or two, a few cocktail tables, some high top tables, as well as a few cocktail musicians and sufficient room for waitstaff and guests to move about.

**This allows for lounge-like seating vignettes, a great big bar, dessert stations, and a dancing area.*

This setup was perfect because the rectangular bar allowed for service on all four sides. It was also fantastic for centralizing the energy in the large room.

On the perimeter of the dance floor,
four large ottomans were positioned
under the oversized fringe shades.
This is a wonderful thing to provide
for guests who don't want to dance
but still want to feel like they are part
of the party.

SCALED FOR IMPACT

I'm a stickler for creating focal points. That's usually accomplished by playing with proportion and scale. If you have a big room, don't think small and fussy. Think large impact. In fact, if you have a small room, think large impact—just with fewer elements. Your goal is to make an impression, and small things just don't register. You've probably noticed I like trees. Why? Because they have great presence. They can also help define a given space. I also like big ottomans (the ones we used for Liz and Kevin's reception could seat six people!), big art/ signs, masses of flowers, and big, long tables, where appropriate. Liz and Kevin's ballroom was huge, so even when we aimed to create intimacy, we did it on a large scale: note the hanging red silk lampshades—they're huge, and in perfect proportion with the room so as to be noticed and not get lost.

ACCENTUATE THE POSITIVE AND MINIMIZE THE NEGATIVE

1. If the venue has a lot of architectural details, such as elaborate molding or fireplaces, keep the tables clean and simple and let the venue have the attention. If the venue is more plain-Jane with bare walls, make it all about the exquisite tables.

2. Though not an absolute, symmetry is a good thing to shoot for to give the room balance.

3. Hate the carpet? Fill the room so you don't see much of it and dim the lights.

4. Hate the drapes? Again, darken the room or steer lights to the center. You can always bring in your own drapes or, even easier, simply ask the venue to take theirs down. In either case, if you are using the room in the evening, you will see very little of them.

5. If the venue comes with its own decorations, such as fake flowers, get rid of them. They will spoil the effect you are trying to achieve.

DESIGNING OUTSIDE THE BOX

Liz and Kevin's venue was wonderfully grand and had many architectural elements in its favor, such as columns and dramatic windows. But the venue had a tried-and-true layout we were expected to follow, which was essentially the traditional horseshoe of round tables around a dance floor. I knew we could do better. When a reception is being planned, there's a tendency to think only in terms of dinner and dancing. The assumption is if you're not eating, you're dancing. I urge you to see the night from your guests' perspective. What if your guest feels stuck at his or her table? Or wishes to socialize with other people? Maybe they simply want to feel part of the room's energy but not necessarily dance. (This can be true for a lot of older guests.) For these reasons, I like to create destination areas that go between dinner and dancing. It's important these areas be in the same room so that you don't risk zapping the energy by splitting the crowd. In this case, we created one long, four-sided bar so that people could mill all around it, as well as huge upholstered ottomans for the corners of the dance floor. The idea is that guests can leave their tables and still stay in the room—rather than seeking refuge elsewhere, such as in the hallway or outside, or even worse, simply leaving the wedding early. It's a total buzz kill when your guests start leaving before the reception has ended.

Liz and Kevin sat with their party and families at a table in the center of the layout. As the bridal couple, you are both the hosts and the honorees. Therefore you should sit among your guests, not apart from them. Weddings are about the unification of two people and two families, and it seems unnatural to put yourself on your own island for the first meal of your married life. If family circumstances make sitting together uncomfortable, sit with friends. Weddings are about together-ness, not separation.

TABLE TALK

As you look at Liz and Kevin's room, among the first things you notice are the rectangular tables. By now, you've probably figured out that, in general, I love rectangular tables. Typically, venues offer two or three sizes of round tables. While there isn't anything wrong with that, there's nothing great about it either. Round tables typically limit the maximum guests per table to ten or twelve. But more important, round tables over 60 inches in diameter don't allow for comfortable conversation. You're stuck talking to just the people on either side of you for the entire reception. And because of the large size, these round tables usually require a considerable centerpiece to fill the space. Rectangular tables are more intimate because they place the person across from you at least 2 feet closer than if you were sitting at a round table. Rectangular tables also give you more options for floral and design arrangements. Instead of the typical floral centerpiece, rectangular tables give you the opportunity to create a tablescape composed of diverse elements. Of course, there's no one, hard-and-fast rule. Round tables have their place; I love them for garden and cocktail parties. Square tables are terrific for a clean, modern effect. My point is that you should think about your tables and use them to enhance the overall room design. This decision can be the single most important factor in the look and feel of the space.

CHAIRS
SITTING
PRETTY

Chairs matter. You see more of them than anything else in the room. Confession time: I really dislike stackable convention chairs, and unfortunately most venues use them. You know the ones: sometimes they are upholstered in stick-to-your-skin pleather, other times in a stained velvet. Nothing kills the look of a room faster than a sea of these chairs. If the chairs are unsightly, it's better to skimp on flowers and rent chairs instead. You can rent just about any kind of chair, but ballroom chairs are the easiest and most common rental. You may prefer them in natural wood, as opposed to painted white or gold, but you don't always get a choice. Consider slipcovering them. Many rental companies offer simple caps or "tuxedos" for chairs (the front stops at the seat and the back is long) along with tie-on cushions. If you're the handy type, you may even sew your own caps to coordinate with your table linens. Or you can have them made. It's worth the effort, believe me. And don't be shy about mixing and matching. Consider using two or three different shades of the same color, as we did for Liz and Kevin's wedding, or go for complete color contrast.

LOCAL COLOR

EVERY TOWN HAS SOMETHING UNIQUE ABOUT IT.

Think about incorporating some of its elements into your day. After all, where you choose to live says a lot about you. New York City is iconic in so many ways, but for Liz and Kevin's wedding, the more obvious references were too cliché.

LIZ SADLER AND KEVIN CRYAN
SEPTEMBER 17, 2005
NEW YORK CITY

ROOMS HAVE BEEN RESERVED FOR OUR GUESTS AT THE FOLLOWING HOTELS. WHEN MAKING RESERVATIONS, PLEASE SPECIFY
THE SADLER-CRYAN WEDDING. TO ENSURE RATES AND AVAILABILITY, PLEASE MAKE RESERVATIONS BY SEPTEMBER 3RD.

DYLAN HOTEL	W HOTEL - THE COURT	THE PIERRE
52 East 41st Street	130 East 39th Street	Two East 61st Street
212.338.0500	212.685.1100	212.838.8000
$185 per evening	$285 per evening	$395 per evening

The save-the-date cards featured something that was signature New York City in a *Saturday Night Live* way: two black-and-white photos in motion—one a taxi and the other a subway, each with Liz and Kevin's names and upcoming wedding date inconspicuously worked in. It was subtle and fun. The photos were made into labels and placed onto gift bags. The result: a distinctly New York wedding, coming and going.

GUEST APPRECIATION

People have to make an effort to attend a wedding. Naturally, those who go to the expense of flying into town and staying at a hotel are the most obvious examples. But even local friends and family have to rearrange their plans, shop for clothes to wear, and perhaps hire a babysitter. Older people have their own sets of needs too, such as having to navigate stairs with a walker. The point is, you should go out of your way to think about everyone's needs and let them know you care. Here are some suggestions:

~ Send a gift bag to any guests staying at hotels. Include a welcome note, a map of the city, and any thoughtful item that will bring a smile, even something as small as a bag of local candy or some fruit.

~ Speak with your caterer or banquet manager and stress that you really would like your guests taken care of. How a guest is treated by the staff is an important part of the experience. Knowing you care can make the staff care, too.

~ Make sure your caterer has vegetarian options.

~ Try to sit older people near the dance floor so they feel a part of the festivities. Younger people will make their way to the dance floor from wherever they are seated.

~ Ask a good friend to look out for a widowed relative or someone who is alone, and maybe even ask them to share a quick dance. With all the distraction, it's easy for vulnerable people to be neglected.

~ Write a warm, personal note in your program or menu thanking everyone for coming and being part of your day.

Half the guests received the subway save-the-date cards, while the other half received the taxi save-the-dates. But all of them had the red back with the hotel information.

AUTUMN IN NEW YORK

Liz and Kevin's wedding did not have a particular theme, but it did have a look. The day took place in September, and given Liz's love of the color red, she opted to saturate the room with rich fall color and textures. Many shades of red on the chair and table linens complemented the venue's dramatic gold drapery. In addition to the linens, the fall harvest atmosphere played out in myriad ways.

LEAF MOTIF
We created a wedding motif featuring a pair of gold leaves and used it on invitations, ceremony programs, and menu cards. It was pretty, romantic, and a nice punctuation to anything it touched.

HARVEST TABLESCAPE
Besides a rich assortment of fall flowers, the tables were lavished with an abundant harvest of elements, including everything from grapes to artichokes to lemon topiaries. Glass hurricane lamps with candles and tall pillars with garlands cascading on distressed bronze holders created a sense of height, old-fashioned romance, and warmth.

CAKE
The five-tiered square cake had a modern sensibility which reflected Liz. The bottom of each tier was designed with a wide ruby ribbon and nail heads, which was a detail from the dinner table linen. Then it was garnished with sugared hydrangea petals from pinks to ruby red.

*We had three bagpipers perform
right outside of the church
immediately following the ceremony.*

REMEMBRANCE
OF THOSE PASSED

Almost inevitably, every couple has a deceased loved one they wish could have been at their wedding. For Kevin, it was his father. Wonderfully enough, Kevin came up with a way to make his dad a part of his day. After the church wedding ceremony, Kevin asked us to arrange to have authentic bagpipe music played, a tradition his father loved. The reflective moment was beautiful and hit just the right tone. I love such an inclusion of the departed—within limits, of course. A wedding is a time to celebrate. It is not a memorial, and you never want to get carried away with a long drawn-out rumination that leaves everyone crying. Instead, like Kevin, you want to think of a tribute that is small and joyous. We worked on a wedding in the Caribbean where three sisters put a candle on a small boat and let it set sail in celebration of their grandmother. It was a lovely gesture. Believe me, your loved ones wouldn't want to be the cause of tears on your big day; they'd rather be a touching presence, even if no one knows but the two of you.

TAKE IT OUTSIDE

4

I LOVE OUTDOOR WEDDINGS

Who doesn't? There's something magical about taking vows in a natural setting with Mother Nature as your witness: the open skies, fresh air, and sheer beauty of it all. Of course, there are as many variations as there are climates, whether as grand as a mountaintop or as intimate as your own backyard. We've done many beach weddings and many countryside ones as well. Outdoor weddings are usually born of a passion for a particular locale. You love the ocean. You love to ski together. You love your home and want to share it with your friends. It's not a casual decision, and for that reason, it's undeniably personal and distinct. Like anything worthwhile, however, it's all in the planning and, most important, your attitude.

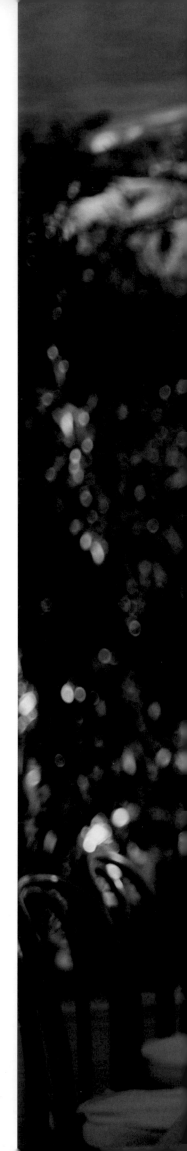

The bride's bouquet—an exquisite arrangement of lilies of the valley—rests by her seat.

I won't pretend outdoor weddings are as easy as renting a ballroom and setting up tables. Indoors provides a certain predictability that outdoors will never give you. However, don't let the element of surprise deter you. Instead, embrace it and appreciate the inherent sense of adventure. You have to start with your fantasy and tailor it for your reality. With an outdoor wedding, you need some built-in contingency plans in case the weather doesn't cooperate. Anticipate wind, rain, and unseasonable weather, be it unusually chilly or extremely hot. All of these things can be accommodated. You can anchor seating cards on the table or a tree; get outdoor heaters or overhead fans; or hand out umbrellas or shawls for the women. The point is, you just have to think of these potentially needed items in advance and have them on hand, even if you never use them. You need to conceptualize a full weather-backup plan for every stage of the wedding and be comfortable with it. Once your day arrives, however, the best plan is to go with the flow and let the professionals working on your behalf make the right calls.

THE STORY OF

Natalia and Todd

Natalia and Todd are both in their 30s. Natalia comes from a close-knit Italian family, with many friends and relatives still in Italy. Refreshingly unpretentious, she is a teacher who has also worked in her family's jewelry business. Todd is a Wall Street trader and shares Natalia's love and respect for family. They had spent many wonderful weekends at the summer home of Natalia's mother in New York's Hudson River Valley, so the home became a very clear choice as a site for their wedding. The two points they and their families kept repeating during the planning process were that they wanted a low-key wedding and they wanted everyone to be comfortable and well cared for, guests and staff alike. The last point mattered most. Given the guest list, which numbered 250, it was clear we would have to take the affair outdoors. And what outdoors they were! Natalia's mother lives in the most glorious of country settings, with lots of rolling hills and a poetic pond. The plan: to embrace the ground's natural beauty at every turn, strategically lighting the pond and the many magnificent trees. Mother Nature should have been a glorious backdrop; instead she insisted on being front and center at all times.

Escort cards pinned on moss
capture the feel of the countryside
at the wedding reception.

INTIMATE CEREMONY, LARGE RECEPTION

Don't fall into the trap of thinking that everyone invited to the reception has to be invited to the ceremony. They don't. Natalia and Todd had their hearts set on marrying at a local clapboard church, practically the size and sweetness of a doll's house. I strongly encouraged them—as I do you—to get married where you want. Two things will prevent any awkwardness or hurt feelings for those who aren't invited to the ceremony:

WORDING ON INVITATIONS

The ceremony invitees receive your classic wedding wording, whereas the reception guests are invited to "a celebration of the marriage" between you and your intended.

ARRIVAL TIMES

As always, timing is everything: you must ensure that the ceremony guests are at the reception site well before the reception-only invitees arrive. Here's why: the last thing you want is to have the reception-only people waiting for you to arrive and enduring groups of people coming in who have clearly just come from the ceremony. Instead, you want reception-only people to be greeted by a cocktail party in full swing. You have complete control over this. For example, we had the ceremony crowd promptly in the tents by 5:15, as the reception crowd was scheduled to arrive at 5:30. Trust me, this seemingly small detail pays off by way of a great first impression.

tent walls were custom built to
extend the home for cocktails. A
marquis connected to a smaller foyer
tent, which then connected to the
clear-span dinner tent. We like to do
this because you see the design in
stages — it feels more residential.

TENTING OUT

Outdoor weddings can be the ultimate "raw" space, which is what makes them deceptively costly. You must bring in everything, starting with the walls and ceilings. You have to plan for rain, meaning you must provide enough cover for all of your guests during the ceremony (assuming it's on-site), cocktails, dinner, and dancing—or at least have an alternative to open skies, just in case. Therefore, outdoor planning begins with the tent. In my book, there is only one absolute rule about tents: they must be laid out very carefully. Besides the main tent(s), you have many additional elements to consider and lay out, such as the cocktail space, walkways, bathrooms, cook tent, and provisions for air conditioning/heat. They can't look like they were just plopped down from the last wedding or event. Mind you, I don't like anything that looks just plopped down, but you particularly don't want to skimp when it comes to something as important as your tent. At the very least, a quality supplier will have clean, well-maintained products. I always insist the tents we use be new, or at least look like they are.

UNDER THE BIG TENT
When it comes to tents, bear in mind these considerations:

~ Flooring levels the ground. In some cases it elevates the tent, which means you need stairs/steps. Make sure the stairway is safe and comfortable for older guests. Wide, gracious steps are always a good choice.

~ Air conditioning or heat: will you need it? Where do the ducts enter the tent? Will they be blowing on guests or blowing out the candles? Ideally, have them run under and enter the tent via the floor, which is the most discreet.

~ The cook tent should be as close as possible to the dining tent to keep the food hot and the service fast.

~ Bathroom trailers should be easily accessible for both cocktails and reception. Ask yourself if you need two of them. These are delivered during the week. Once in place, they are very difficult to move, which is why you need to make sure they are dropped off in the right space.

THE GREENHOUSE EFFECT
Natalia and Todd's wedding required two main tents: a rectangular one for dinner and a great round one for dancing and dessert. The rectangular one was inspired by the house's original greenhouse. This clear-span tent was designed with a see-through vinyl top and Plexiglas sides to let in as much of the outdoors as possible, given the early evening hour. We added some touches to complete the look.

TENTS DELIBERATELY BUILT NEAR TREES
To create the romantic feeling of dining in an enchanted forest, the tent was tucked underneath enormous tree branches. These branches helped suggest a canopy.

Festive round dessert and dance tent.
Silk fabric panels make the tent rich
and the paper lanterns make it fun.
Great atmosphere for a wonderful party!

TENT IN THE ROUND

The round tent chosen for dancing and dessert involved some serious construction, including leveling the floor on a sloping hill. Three circumference levels were created (almost like an upside-down wedding cake) to give the space interest and dimension. There were a number of other things used to enhance the atmosphere.

 **A BAND IN WHITE JACKETS** Much of the music played was big band and swing, which is why it felt very glamorous and nostalgic to have the band wear white dinner jackets. Moreover, the band became a focal point of the room.

~ **DRAPED PANELS** What better way to fight an otherwise cavernous space? Draped panels created focus and intimacy. The red color gave the space a warmth and lushness.

~ **DOZENS OF PAPER LANTERNS** You may have noticed that I'm a big fan of paper lanterns. They give any room instant drama, elegance, and graphic appeal. Lighting doesn't come any cheaper or more versatile. Best of all, you can shine a color on them and they will look completely different—plus you can recycle them at your next event. Dining or dancing under an abundance of paper lanterns is instant fun and romance.

WEATHER PERMITTING
HOPE FOR THE BEST, PLAN FOR THE WORST

No one can predict the weather, not even the pros. This was an October wedding where the area's average nightly temperature is usually between 35 and 40 degrees. However, a warm front combined with high humidity made the rehearsal dinner too warm. Fortunately, a cold front came rushing in right around the time the wedding started. Unfortunately, the cold front was accompanied by rain—and not a light sprinkle. In 24 hours, 10 inches of rain fell, more than ever recorded in such a time frame. Canceling the wedding was not an option. So we went with the flow, keeping what plans we could, coming up with alternatives for those we couldn't, and forgetting some altogether (such as lighting the pond and trees). There were plenty of last-minute adaptations (including a few caused by a temporary power outage!), but not one of them ruined the day. In fact, we all agreed that the torrential downpour created a unique intimacy and instant camaraderie. Spirits were high, and we were all happy to be in this together.

THE BEST-LAID PLANS
No one *counts* on rain. Instead, you envision clear, sunny skies and perfect temperatures—as we did for this wedding. Here are a few examples of what we originally planned and what we actually did.

~ Original Plan: To have cars parked on a grass field by a valet.
Contingency Plan: Set up a valet on the main road at a large gas station parking lot where the cars wouldn't sink into the lawn. Used the gas station's canopy as the transfer site to keep guests dry. The family's antique cars shuttled guests to the reception site.

~ Original Plan: To have cocktails outdoors where guests could wander the property, set up with tables, umbrellas, and clay chimneys (for warmth).
Contingency Plan: Had a mover on standby to clear out furniture. Connected large tents to the home, creating a large indoor-outdoor cocktail space. Lit the fireplace and built a large, drive-through tent in front of the house so people could be dropped off without getting wet.

~ Original Plan: To have open-air walks between tents.
Contingency Plan: Had connecting "halls" constructed between the two tents. All tents were connected seamlessly.

To make the guests feel like they were dining outside, we placed the clear-span tent under the enormous trees. Traditional candleholders would have sufficed, but chandeliers made from birchwood, holding fifty votives each, were so much more whimsical and in the spirit of a magical forest.

AT YOUR SERVICE

Whenever you can, try to be considerate of those who are hired to help execute your day. Anticipating the needs of others matters, not only because it's the right thing to do, but also because if you do your best for people they do their best for you.

It's not just guests who need protection from the rain. You also need to supply rain gear for the staff working the wedding. Plan to have lots of golf-sized umbrellas, rain ponchos, and the means to keep all equipment safe and dry.

Natalia's father insisted we provide good meals (the same food that the guests were eating) at a table for many of the key personnel working the wedding. Moreover, we provided appropriate clothes and shoes for the men who were driving the antique cars. It made them look like proper drivers, and also took the pressure off individuals to find appropriate clothing, since they were not required to wear such clothes in their daily lives. The clothes became a keepsake from the wedding.

MANAGING A LARGE-SCALE EVENT

A great event doesn't happen on its own. Every detail is scrupulously planned and each step is carefully orchestrated. For this wedding, we had a team of twelve planners working behind the scenes to make sure all went as smoothly as possible. Of course, you never want your event to feel over-orchestrated. It should feel organic, with each moment seamlessly flowing into the next. It is the invisible planner who should be pulling the strings from behind the curtain, ensuring that a great dance set moves into the main course, which is followed by a heartwarming toast before everyone gets back on the dance floor. For such seamlessness to occur, you need a detailed timeline set up for the entire week as well as a meticulous timeline for the actual day. Each staff member should have his or her orders and be responsible for specific elements. Ironically, being fully prepared this way is what frees you to deal with the unexpected, however small or great it may be.

A round tent was used for dancing and dessert. Three tiers allowed for a seating area with cushions, various bars, and a generous dance floor.

BABIES
ON BOARD

Here's another tip I highly recommend. If you can, provide on-site babysitting services for people with young children (under 12). Many young parents don't have access to a good weekend/nighttime babysitter and come to your wedding anxious about their children at home. These parents can't relax and have a good time. However, if their children are in the next room, the mother or father can occasionally check on them and come back to the reception with a mind at ease. Natalia and Todd provided such services and, at the end of the night, a few of the children came out to join their parents for a bit before heading home. Should you opt to do this, here are a few suggestions:

~ Babies under 8 months need baby nurses, not just sitters.

~ Provide a kid-friendly menu.

~ Supply a television and some favorite videos.

~ Consider personalized goodie bags. We made bags with the children's names and stocked them with toys, games, crayons, and coloring books.

TAKE
GOOD CARE

I'm big on finding little ways for you to show your guests that you care about them. This wedding could have been a disaster. Had we allowed the guests to get wet, have their cars get stuck in the muddy grass, or have to share umbrellas, the hardship would have been the focus of their night. It doesn't take much to make or break a guest's experience—just some advance planning and very good care.

EMBRACE YOUR HERITAGE

THIS IS A SUBJECT THAT'S NEAR AND DEAR TO ME.

I'm Korean-born and my husband, Josh, is Jewish. One of the most meaningful parts of our wedding day was when we took part in the Peh Beck ceremony. The only surviving rite of the Old Confucian wedding ceremony, this is a Korean ritual where the couple is dressed in traditional garb and engages in several symbolic gestures such as bowing to their elder family members. The groom carries his bride on his back as a symbol of his promise to care for her. The mothers toss gifts of dates and chestnuts, symbols of future children, which the bride tries to catch in her large skirt. This ritual is usually attended only by family and very close friends, so we purposely scheduled it during the cocktail hour in a separate room. Little did we know that when the word got out what we were doing, all of our guests wanted to bear witness. The cocktail hour went on far longer than planned.

People love culture in all its forms. They like to learn and partake in rituals, especially when they are joyful, such as wedding ceremonies. This is your chance to honor and share where you are from, who you are now, and the family you will be together. America is a wonderful melting pot of traditions and culture. (Religion is often an important part of one's culture, but here I'm referring specifically to more ethnic or regional culture.) Culture is what makes us unique; it's also what people remember. There are caveats, however. You never want to make someone feel uncomfortable or out of place. Unless you are a part of a very insular group, where all your family and guests are of your same background, you have to embrace culture with sensitivity and consideration. You wouldn't enjoy yourself at a wedding where everyone spoke Italian except you, or where everyone was in on a ritual and you had no idea what was going on, much less what was expected of you. Your approach should always be one of celebration and inclusion. The goal is to create an experience where everyone leaves feeling a bit richer for it.

THE STORY OF

Herran and Sam

Herran and Sam, both 31, make a striking couple. She is of Ethiopian descent and he Norwegian. The two went to high school together, yet it wasn't until their 10-year reunion that sparks flew. From that point, they were inseparable, despite living on different coasts, she being a news producer in New York and he a comedy writer in Los Angeles. Herran moved to L.A., and soon afterward they got engaged. But they knew that they wanted to get married in New York, where both their families live. The couple had a huge advantage going for them: their families loved one another and were happy to pitch in with the long-distance planning. In fact, the two mothers-in-law spent a whole day with us just looking for venues. I can't remember another set of in-laws so vastly different from each other yet so full of mutual admiration and respect. The bride and groom each had one sister; his sister was the "best woman" and hers the maid of honor. Adding to the familial lovefest, Sam's aunt officiated the ceremony. You really felt theirs was a marriage of two families, not just two people. Style-wise, Herran and Sam's direction was clear and simple: this was a modern couple who wanted few frills and lots of sophistication for their 250 guests. It was also important to Herran to pay homage to her heritage and share it with her new family and all the couple's friends.

A WELL-ORCHESTRATED EVENING

Some weddings are more casual than others. A wedding as complex as this one, however, could leave little to chance. Seating 250 people around five long tables (the tables spanned two city blocks!) required much advanced planning in terms of seating and escorting guests to those seats. The more elaborate the wedding concept, the more you have to anticipate the various logistics. Guests should never be confused as to where they need to go and when. Try to envision the night from their point of view and plan accordingly. More staff may be required to help guide your guests and keep the evening on schedule.

LOCATION MATTERS

I hope you're starting to get a sense of why it doesn't pay to rush into a location. You need to first figure out what matters most to you and then go about finding a reception space to accommodate as many of those elements as possible. We wanted a place with a sense of history and multiple rooms properly sized to host three different stages of the wedding: cocktails, a dining room that would fit 250 people at a single table, and then dancing and dessert. Instead of considering the usual locations, we focused on unique spaces that rented their facilities for events. We ended up at The New York Public Library. We loved the stone walls and the high ceilings. We also loved the history, architecture, and grandness of it. Turning it into a dining/dancing space wasn't easy, but our efforts were well rewarded as it proved to be a truly magical event. In each city, I urge you to research not-so-obvious location options, which can include public spaces, lobbies of old buildings, private clubs, photo studios, art galleries, and places that defy categorization.

WHAT'S SO GREAT ABOUT PUBLIC BUILDINGS?

Take a drive through town and keep your mind open. Banks, libraries, town halls, marinas, botanical gardens—many offer themselves as wedding venues. On the downside, you often have to bring in every element and coordinate the deliveries and setup. But don't let that stand in your way; it's well worth the effort. Here's why I love public spaces.

THEY'RE GRANDLY DESIGNED
Think high ceilings, marble or stone walls.

THEY HAVE CHARACTER
Usually because they are older than most buildings.

THEY'RE UNEXPECTED
Unusual places make for special weddings.

THEY'RE ACCESSIBLE
Most are located in the center of town.

THEY FEEL IMPORTANT
The scale makes them feel notable, as if they were built to last forever.
Like your marriage.

PLANNING A WEDDING FROM AFAR

Though the wedding was in New York, Herran and Sam live full time in Los Angeles. They had us and their mothers to help them, but there were still many decisions to be made long distance. Herran was only able to fly into New York a few times in advance. Thanks to the Internet, information is much easier to obtain wherever you are; the trick is not to waste a lot of time during those in-person visits. Below are some helpful hints if you find yourself in a similar position.

BE EFFECTIVE AND EFFICIENT BEFORE COMING TO TOWN

Do as much research online as possible. Find out all that you can, such as price, availability, or room size. Ask vendors to email you pictures. Anything you can find out in advance is that much time you are saving when you arrive. If a meeting isn't scheduled before your trip, the odds are it won't happen.

ORGANIZE YOURSELF

Your planning time is limited. Buy notebooks and binders dedicated to your wedding. Create a travel plan, and always have a master contact sheet on hand, so you have numbers and addresses on you at all times. If you aren't working with a planner, enlist a family member or friend to go on appointments with you for another pair of eyes and ears.

SCHEDULE YOUR MEETINGS ACCORDING TO LOCATION

Plan for an hour per meeting. Recognize that travel time eats up a lot of the day, so try to cluster appointments that are near one another.

ASK VENDORS ABOUT OTHER VENDORS

If you like a hotel or restaurant, ask who does their flowers. When you encounter someone whose taste you trust, ask for an opinion on other local talent. Yes, there is always some back-scratching that goes on among vendors and venues, but the more you ask, hopefully, the more you will see the same names reappearing. If someone is mentioned by several people, it is usually a good sign.

MAKE YOUR MEETINGS PURPOSEFUL

Do as much prescreening as you can before the trip so that you can use the meeting time to dive into the details of your wedding. Make sure you have questions in hand for the actual appointment. Have a notepad with you, and write down all impressions during and pertinent information immediately following the meeting. (Don't leave it to memory as it all blurs together after a busy day.) Also, bring any information and images that you can share in order to give these people a good sense of what you are thinking for your wedding.

Sam sees his beautiful bride for the first time. They enjoy a precious moment by themselves on the spectacular roofdeck overlooking Central Park.

PHOTO EXPRESS
CONSIDER TAKING YOUR PHOTOS BEFORE THE CEREMONY

Tradition has it that it's bad luck to see your intended before the ceremony. I respect anyone who upholds those beliefs, but I'm not one of them. In fact, I went with this tradition and it is among my few regrets about my wedding. I thought we would be robbed of the moment of my husband seeing me for the first time as I walked down the aisle. Experience with my clients tells me that in this instance, you can have your cake and eat it, too. There are many good reasons to buck the trend and have your photos taken before you do anything else.

YOU'RE AT YOUR PHOTO BEST
Your hair is in place, your makeup freshly applied. You also aren't emotionally distracted with the recent ceremony or people wanting your attention.

YOU CAN ENJOY YOUR COCKTAIL HOUR AND KEEP THE RECEPTION ON TRACK
Cocktail hour is the ideal time to greet your guests and accept their congratulations. You are the hosts, and this is your first opportunity to act the part. Family photos almost always take longer than expected, meaning that couples, their families, and the bridal party often miss a lot or all of their cocktail hour.

YOU CAN ARRANGE TO HAVE THAT MAGICAL FIRST MOMENT BETWEEN THE TWO OF YOU
Understandably, you don't want to miss that first moment your husband sees you on your wedding day. People are sensitive to this. Simply arrange through your photographer or planner to see each other for the first time where you will be taking photos. Usually the bride is positioned where the groom can come around the corner and see her for the first time. It is a highly emotional moment which can be treasured privately or with close family.

PHOTOGRAPHY BEFOREHAND ALLOWS YOU TO RELAX AND BETTER ENJOY THE CEREMONY
Couples often tell us that seeing each other before the ceremony calms their nerves and allows them to enjoy the ceremony much more. Your wedding ceremony is such a treasured part of your life that you want to be in the moment as much as possible.

IT FREES YOU TO TAKE A FEW MINUTES ALONE TOGETHER AFTER THE CEREMONY
Your emotions directly after the ceremony are unlike any other in your life. I highly encourage taking a few minutes to enjoy them in privacy.

CEREMONIAL ADVICE

ENJOY IT AND TAKE IT ALL IN

Herran was an especially beautiful bride, in part because of her amazing glow. This was a woman in love, and you could see it as she walked down the aisle. Most brides are so nervous that a kind of stage fright comes over them, and they forget to appreciate the joy of the moment. I was such a bride. I was intent on not making a mistake. Because of that, I've learned to urge my clients to breathe deeply, hold their heads high, and keep their shoulders straight. Look your guests in the eyes and appreciate just how wondrous the ceremony is. Take it all in. Don't be afraid to smile at your guests, much less your intended. This is your moment. Enjoy it for all it is worth.

BOUND TOGETHER, ETHIOPIAN STYLE

While Herran and Sam's ceremony wasn't of any particular ethnic tradition, they shared a beautiful moment. A few years back, Herran traveled to Ethiopia where she was baptized in a *shamma*, a traditional shawl made of fine cotton. For their wedding ceremony, the two joined hands and the *shamma* was wrapped around their hands, binding them together for life.

A MODERN TAKE ON A CLASSIC SETTING

After our day of location scouting, the two mothers-in-law recommended The New York Public Library. Herran and Sam agreed. Since we knew Herran and Sam liked all things modern, we decided to go with a minimal décor. We stuck to shades of stone (to match the white marble) and simple white flowers, including modern arrangements behind the bar, and dramatic, blooming white cherry branches to punctuate the five 44-foot-long tables. On the tables, we added just a few colorful punches of tangerine and café au lait through roses, sweet peas, colored mini callis, and sunburst menu cards. The chairs were sleek and modern dark gray Philippe Starck Bellinis. I love the juxtaposition of the old and the new. You appreciate the grandeur of such a space even more when you keep it clean and simple.

Seat cushions warm the cold marble bench. Simple modern Parsons tables, individual white blossoms, and votive candles make this seating more inviting.

CHRISTOPHER RYLEY 5E
LUCINDA RYLEY 2W
MARCUS SAMUELSSON 2W
THOMAS SAUNDERS 1E
MARIA SHINDLER 5W
ANTHONY SCHLOSS 5W
MARIZA SCOTCH 2W
NICK SCRUGGS 5E
GUSTAV SEELBINDER 4E
JUNO SHAYE 5E
NARDOS SHIFEROW 4E
SIKITA SKINNER 4E
JANE STENEHJEM 4W
JOSH SUNIEWICK 2E
MAGGIE SUNIEWICK 2E
YASUKO TAMAKI 1W
ANNE TATLOCK 4W

ESCORT ELEGANCE

FAR LEFT: *Guests' names were silk-screened onto banners to guide them to their seats. The W or E told them if they were on the west or east side, which was important to know because the tables were so long.* LEFT: *Pencils and composition books allowed guests to record their good wishes.* RIGHT: *The cake was topped with a book showing a Shakespearean sonnet that reflected Herran and Sam's love of literature. Of course it was all edible!*

TIGHT ON SPACE, LONG ON WALLS

You've no doubt noticed I like to play with escort tables. Here's why: at some point, every guest will seek out a seating assignment. Before you plop a floral arrangement on a round white table, use your imagination to come up with something different. In this case, there was no logical place for a table and we needed to screen off the cocktail area from the dinner room. But the walls were amazing to work with. The solution was a 12-by-12-foot museum-styled banner that listed the guests' names with corresponding table IDs. To underscore the point, the font matched the inscriptions on the wall. Although it looks effortless in the picture—believe me—it wasn't easy to produce. I had to find a printer who could print on large fabric without any seams and then do a series of calculations as to how big the type should be and where to begin it so the people at the top of the list could see their names effortlessly, too. It was also important the type look like the library font. If there's a will, there's always a way. You just have to find it. Guests laughed about how it looked like they were big contributors to the library. It was very cool for them to see their names in such a permanent-looking context.

LITERARY TOUCHES

Culture isn't just ethnicity. It's also how you live and express yourself. In so many ways, Herran and Sam were people of words: they met at school—he had been a schoolteacher and was now a writer. And this was The New York Public Library, after all. We added some subliminal touches to underscore the point: old-fashioned composition books and no. 2 pencils for guest sign-ins; a wedding cake topped with a "book" opened to a Shakespearean sonnet; as favors, homemade cookies wrapped in a vintage print of stacked books.

COCKTAILS: A TIME FOR MUSICAL CHAIRS

Cocktails are a time to mix it up. People can mill about, meeting and talking to guests who won't be at their table. The same holds true for the music. If you have a specific genre of music you enjoy, bring it out for the cocktail hour. Sam was a big jazz enthusiast. He was especially passionate about Charles Mingus, the great American jazz composer. After Mingus's passing, his wife kept his legacy alive through the Charles Mingus Band, a premiere jazz ensemble. While a genre-specific band would never work for the reception, it worked just beautifully for the cocktail hour. This is yet another example of a couple sharing something that was personal and meaningful to them.

An extraordinary dinner in
a magnificent setting was incredibly
intimate in feel because guests felt
like they were all sharing the same
spectactular table. It was almost
two city blocks long!

INTERNATIONAL CUISINE

No matter what your ethnic persuasion, your wedding is not the time to introduce a whole new palette of tastes to your guests. Many people don't like and won't eat unfamiliar food because they worry it won't agree with them. However, you can offer more than an all-or-nothing proposition. I urge you to add a taste of your culture, especially if it's unique fare. At Herran and Sam's wedding, the meal began with a sampler of traditional Ethiopian dishes. (We enlisted a favorite Ethiopian restaurant who worked with the wedding's main caterer.) Four selections were served, accompanied by *injera*, the indigenous bread of Ethiopia, and homemade Ethiopian honey wine. This food is designed to be eaten with your hands and shared family-style with those around you. It was a hit. The Ethiopian guests loved the familiarity of the food, while the American guests loved the exoticism of trying something new.

GO AUTHENTIC

You want to present unusual food with integrity and in its best light. Serve it in its traditional style, with the corresponding utensils (or lack thereof), and have it prepared by someone who knows what they're doing. Don't ask an American caterer to create ethnic food from a recipe; chances are the taste will be off. If you opt to go to a restaurant, be respectful and inclusive of your caterer. We all know what happens when too many chefs are in the kitchen.

INCLUDE A DESCRIPTION/EXPLANATION ON THE MENU CARD

Even the most intrepid diners want to know what they're eating, especially if they have allergies or other dietary concerns. Also, it's simply more fun to understand the origin of and the tradition behind what's being served.

APPRECIATE THAT IT'S NOT FOR EVERYONE

Some will love the chance to taste new food, others won't even try it. That's what makes the world go round. Don't take it personally.

ENSURE THAT THE MENU IS DIVERSIFIED

You have to consider people who skip exotic fare and make sure they will still have enough to eat. You don't want anyone to go home hungry.

HERE'S TO A GOOD TOAST

Herran and Sam's families gave some truly touching toasts to one another and their guests. A few toasts elicited tears because they were so beautiful. Weddings are a time for toasting. Yet you'd be surprised how many people don't rehearse, opting to just stand up and wing it. A toast is a serious thing. You're saying something that will live on in many a memory. As bride and groom, at least one of you will want to stand up and thank everyone for coming.

RECOGNIZE THAT IT IS, IN FACT, PUBLIC SPEAKING
Speak slowly and clearly. Follow long sentences with short ones. Most of all, rehearse what you plan to say in front of a mirror as well as in front of an honest friend. Every time you practice your speech, it will improve.

WORDS MATTER
A wedding is a momentous occasion, so the words should have meaning. Be sincere and respectful and speak from your heart. Also, remember always to be inclusive. You're not just speaking to one another, your families, or people who are in on a particular joke. Make everyone feel you're speaking to them as well.

WRITE IT DOWN
As with any message, you need to have a beginning, middle, and end. This is not the time to free associate. If you can, memorize it. If you can't, consider a cue card that reminds you of your key points. Try to avoid reading it from a crumpled piece of paper.

KEEP IT BRIEF
Even a good speech quickly becomes a bore if it goes on too long. Well-chosen words have lasting impact. Three to five minutes is ideal.

BE YOURSELF
Speak with your usual style and language. Now's not the time to bring out the S.A.T. words. They will sound unnatural. Most important, it's okay to be nervous. Just speak from the heart; that's all that matters. Everything connected to a wedding should come from the heart, and it will all be right.

SPEAK INTO THE MICROPHONE
It won't matter how good your speech is if nobody hears it. Most microphones won't pick up the speaker's voice unless the mouth is less than an inch from the microphone.

GET INTIMATE

There are many reasons to have a small wedding besides the monetary one. One of you could be shy and therefore uncomfortable being the center of attention in front of a large group. The thought of having a couple hundred people overwhelms you. You may have a small family or a family that lives far away and therefore only a few of them are able to attend. You may have a list so large that you have to diplomatically cut off certain categories altogether, for example, no work friends or second cousins. Perhaps it's your second wedding and therefore you'd prefer a more modest reception. Or just as common,

you simply may desire to join your lives together with just the closest people in your lives as witnesses.

Whatever your reason and whatever the size of your wedding, you still want it to be as special as your relationship. I define small as a guest list of up to one hundred people. We've done smaller weddings, including a thirty-five-person dinner party. The fun part about planning a small wedding is that you can be flexible in many ways. You can host the wedding in a smaller space or move from room to room. You can also specialize the food in a way that is far more difficult to do with a larger crowd. Trust me, a limited guest list doesn't necessarily mean less planning or huge savings; it just means the freedom to really think outside the box and take your guests on a very special journey.

THE STORY OF

Marcy and Rick

Marcy, a schoolteacher in her late 20s, and Rick, a businessman in his mid-40s, knew exactly what they wanted for their wedding: a small gathering of their most beloved friends and family—no more than one hundred people, tops. Family included Rick's two grown daughters, who walked him down the aisle. (Marcy's brother did the honors for her.) The couple was adamant that they wanted to share their favorite food and music. Though they wanted a black-tie affair, they also wanted people to be comfortable and feel really pampered. (Remember, formal does not mean stuffy and boring.) After much searching, we decided on a five-star New York City hotel, a place where Rick had many business meetings. This hotel is not known for its weddings, primarily because of its small event rooms. Given our guest list, that wasn't a problem. In fact, we used it to our advantage, hosting cocktails in one space, the ceremony in another, dinner in a third place, and dessert and dancing in a fourth. Marcy knew she wanted a "white" wedding reception, and Rick's main request was that the familiar hotel be entirely transformed to feel like a new destination, one uniquely their own. Both Marcy and Rick were intimately involved in every aspect of their wedding. No detail was too small to discuss, no element too insignificant to question. As a result, their guests were treated to a night as heavenly as it was indulgent.

HAUTE HOTELS

There are many benefits to choosing a hotel as your venue. First and foremost is its hospitality. You can book a room to get ready or one to spend the night in. There is no traveling on either end of the affair, and therefore no worries. The convenience is just wonderful. You also have a ready-made place for out-of-town guests to stay. And even if you don't require overnight accommodations, many hotels have day rates for the groom in addition to the bridal suite, which is usually included. Most hotels are centrally located, have valet parking, and offer a host of other amenities you can cross off your worry list. On your wedding day, the greatest luxury of all is peace of mind.

DRESSED IN
WHITE

HALLWAY TO HEAVEN

Since Marcy had her heart set on a white wedding, we decided to take it one step further and make the experience positively heavenly. The first step was draping the hallway in white. This created a dramatically ethereal entrance to the ceremony room, almost like walking through clouds. This is an especially great thing to do when you want to mask a sterile walkway or one with fluorescent lighting. Later, when guests traversed the same hallway for dessert and dancing, red gels placed over the lights created more of a nightclub effect.

THERE'S A REASON EVERYONE LOVES WHITE: IT'S SIMPLE AND ELEGANT

In Marcy and Rick's case it was also incredibly chic and sophisticated. In addition to the white-draped hallway, we dressed the ceremony room in sheer organza and had lots and lots of candlelight. Being Jewish but not religious, the couple wanted an "interpretive" chuppah. We created one with white quinces on the corners of the altar and the accompanying aisle. The reception room featured full-length ivory silk slipcovered chairs and table-cloths with huge vases of French tulips as well as clusters of white garden roses, ranunculus, and par-rot tulips. The overall effect was stunning in its clean sophistication.

1. YOU SAVE TIME
A choice of entrée significantly slows down the flow of the evening: once in taking orders (people are never at their seats) and again in serving (it requires more time and space for the kitchen).

2. YOU SAVE MONEY
Choice drives up the cost to the caterer, which is usually passed on to you.

3. GUESTS CAN STILL HAVE WHAT IS CALLED A "SILENT OPTION"
At the bottom of your menu card, guests should be informed that a vegetarian option is available upon request.

4. YOU CAN STILL BE CONSIDERATE
Provide your caterers with any guest preferences, allergies, or eating requirements beforehand. As long as the caterers know early enough, they usually are able to accommodate them. This is the most gracious way to host an event.

THE RIGHTS OF WHITE

White can be absolutely beautiful when done right. Should you decide to go white, especially if that's what the venue is offering, be bold about it. Here are some ideas to enhance white's inherent elegance.

CONSIDER USING A SHEER ORGANZA OVERLAY
Rent or buy a table overlay that has a beautiful embroidered pattern; it can add great textural interest.

USE COLORED OR PRINTED NAPKINS
Again, rent or buy them in bulk. A delicate floral or a sophisticated stripe works wonders on an otherwise all-white table.

EMBRACE THE WHITE
Make it look deliberate by selecting ivory and white flowers. Layer ecru and other naturals in your linens.

ADD A TONAL RUNNER
Make, buy, or rent them. I love runners, especially on rectangular tables. It defines the table's center and is a perfect frame for your centerpieces.

THE DINNER PARTY APPROACH

The best menus have the care and specialty of a dinner party in your own home or in your favorite restaurant. Admittedly, the smaller the guest list the easier this is to accomplish, either because you can splurge on pricier foods or because it's simpler to prepare more challenging dishes in smaller quantities. Even though Marcy and Rick had a black-tie wedding and the hotel offered haute cuisine, the couple wanted to serve their favorite foods—some even designed to be eaten with hands. For the appetizer, we worked with the hotel's chef to create a tasting plate of the couple's favorite foods. For dinner, they served surf and turf—lobster tails and filet mignon. And for dessert, they pulled out the stops with childhood favorites: brownies, blondies, chocolate chip cookies, cupcakes, and Rice Krispie treats.

The first course of this intimate dinner celebration was the couple's favorite trio—crisp calamari, tomato and mozzarella, and shrimp cocktail—paired with fantastic wine.

LEFT: *First-course appetizer trio of tomato and mozarella, crisp calamari, and shrimp cocktail.* MIDDLE: *Colorful poppy flowers in test tubes with pillar candles for a cozy niche.* RIGHT: *Lucite cocktail table for the cafe during dancing.*

ROOMS
TO MOVE

As mentioned, Marcy and Rick's day was broken into four distinct parts and three rooms, one of which was re-dressed and used again. I'm a big fan of changing rooms throughout the evening. Here's why: one of the biggest complaints I hear about weddings is being stuck at one table for the night. That's a lot of hours to sit in one place, especially if you don't care to dance. By changing rooms, you're inviting guests to go on a journey with you. Each room reveals a new personality and set of circumstances. There's always a surprise and something to look forward to. Keep these points in mind.

Multiple-room receptions work especially well for small weddings. The more people you have, the more logistically difficult it is to move.

Changing rooms isn't great if you have many older guests. Some people need to be seated in one place and have a home base for the evening. Also, it's not fair to keep moving older people if every move is a physical challenge.

If you do opt to switch rooms, know in advance how you will signal to guests that it's time to move, whether it's done by the waitstaff or as an invitation at the end of a speech. Whatever you do, don't use bells. People aren't cows.

Anticipate who will need help getting from one room to another and provide for it.

LIGHTS, CAMERA, ACTION!

Understandably, many bridal couples shudder at the idea of having someone videotape their wedding. We've all been at affairs where the videographer took over with blinding lights, clunky equipment, and—worse yet—a microphone in hand asking you for a special message to the bride and groom as you're trying to eat or have a private conversation. It doesn't have to be that way, I promise. Technology is changing and so is the art of videography. There's no reason why a videographer can't act like a fly on the wall and still get the essence of your wedding. Marcy and Rick resisted hiring a videographer at first and then at the last minute hired someone just to record their ceremony. They were thrilled they'd changed their minds. A document of such an important moment (that otherwise would be a blur in your memory) is something you'll have for the rest of your life.

WHEN INTERVIEWING VIDEOGRAPHERS

1. Make sure to see a full wedding video, not just a demo tape. Videography today is about editing and how the story of your wedding is told. If you like the reel, ask who edited it and if that person can edit yours as well.

2. Ask to see the equipment. Like all technology, video equipment is smaller now, so you want to make sure the videographer has updated his or hers. New digital technology allows video-graphers to shoot with very little light.

3. Find out if the videographer works with one camera or with another person. If the budget allows, two cameramen are ideal because you can get reaction shots.

4. Ask to see their lights and how they would light a setting similar to one you'll be in. If their reel is of outdoor weddings, you won't know how they might handle a candlelit ballroom.

5. You have control. You can instruct your videographer not to ask guests to speak and not to intrude on the dance floor. Remember, this is your movie he's filming.

MUSIC
CREATE A SENTIMENTAL JOURNEY

Marcy and Rick did something novel for their ceremony: they had their favorite contemporary songs recomposed, sans lyrics, using instrumentals featuring guitar, keyboard, percussion, and flute. The result was familiar music recast with a dreamy quality. These were the songs they had fallen in love to, so each had meaning, and you could see everyone smile with recognition as one song flowed into another. Your ceremony music selection needs to have meaning for you. Walk down the aisle to Pachelbel's "Canon" if this is what you've always envisioned. Just don't select it by default. The most important thing is that the song gives you goose bumps as you are preparing to walk down the aisle. Hopefully this will happen every time you hear the song after your wedding. Figuring out what's the perfect ceremony music for you takes time. Don't rush it.

CEREMONY MUSIC
When hiring classical musicians, hire those who have played together frequently. Even if your musicians have played in famous symphonies, you still need them to operate as a cohesive team. The most common problem is that the musicians don't start and stop each song in unison. The more they have played together, the better they pick up the leader's start/stop cues, making these transitions smoother. Also, understand their ability to learn songs if you are considering something nontraditional.

RECEPTION MUSIC
PREPARING THE MUSICAL TALENT FOR YOUR EVENT

MAKE SURE THAT THE DJ OR BANDLEADER UNDERSTANDS THE SONGS AND MUSICAL GENRES YOU LIKE AND DON'T LIKE
The more information you can provide the better. Then trust them to do their thing—don't dictate every song. Each party has its own life and energy. The music needs to adjust to the flow of the event. However, if you discover that you've hired the wrong people to handle your music (which I hope you don't), be firm and tell the band/DJ exactly what to do. Nothing will ruin a great celebration more than a bad band or DJ.

DISCUSS YOUR MUSIC PLAN FOR THE EVENING
Although music rules are meant to be broken, typically the musical journey during the night is chronological, starting with standards and swing and working its way up to current music. During the early stages of the night, you want to play music that will get the older crowd on the dance floor. Standards also give a timeless, romantic feel to the wedding, especially while everyone is first noticing the beautiful décor of the room. Each dance set should build on the previous one, increasing the energy of the night.

WRITE THE DETAILS DOWN FOR YOUR BAND OR DJ
Hand it to them on the day of your wedding. Make sure to include your Do Not Play List, Must Play List, how you would like to be introduced (word for word), special dances and their timing (first dance, father/daughter, mother/son, cake cutting, etc.). I always instruct the bandleader or DJ to speak only when necessary; less is more.

SNEAK SOME SURPRISES INTO THE EVENING
Perhaps you can choose a special song for your new husband, or your parents' wedding song. If it isn't dance music, play it during dinner.

UNCONVENTIONAL WISDOM

Many couples go with convention because they don't want to rock the boat. It's easier to do what's expected of you. Sometimes it's cheaper, too, since the venue doesn't have to reinvent the wheel with every wedding. I've already shown you many examples of couples who personalized their weddings with grand, chic, and/or whimsical touches. But how far can you go? What conventions can you dispense with altogether? At a certain point, will it still feel like a wedding and not just a wonderful, joyous party? To me, it all has to do with the couple and their personal preferences. Sometimes all you want is exactly that—a wonderful, joyous party—which is why some couples choose to elope and throw a party afterward. Other times, you want to embrace every tradition you can think of, and that too is all right, as long as you do it in your own style.

OTHER THAN THE MARRIAGE LICENSE EVERYTHING IS OPEN TO INTERPRETATION

You don't *have* to do anything (other than be considerate hosts). But there are, in fact, many things you'll *want* to do. Many brides won't feel married unless they walk down an aisle. Some won't feel like a bride unless they're wearing white. You really have to ask yourself what traditions are important to you. What will you regret if you *don't* do it? Then you ask yourself the fun questions: What would tickle your fancy? What would really enhance the specialness of the day? How can you create a wedding that is unmistakably yours and yours alone? Those are the answers that will make your wedding a truly memorable affair for you and your guests.

THE STORY OF

Cindy and Ian

Talk about an unconventional couple! You only need hear how Ian, a human rights attorney, proposed to Cindy: he rented a white horse and, wearing head-to-toe metal armor, came charging at her on a beach. Cindy, a successful writer and television producer, was just thrilled by the dramatic gesture. This was Cindy's second marriage and Ian's first. These two 40-year-olds are witty, fun to be with, and full of energy. They longed for their wedding to be as irreverent and wildly romantic as one of Cindy's *Sex and the City* scripts. As hosts, they wanted their friends and family to come, have a great time, and share in their love for each other. The couple had started planning for the wedding on their own, but shortly into the process they realized they needed help. You can be as unconventional as you want, but at the end of the day there are a lot of organizational and practical considerations that get in the way. For example, their wedding was set for June, on one of the longest days of the year. Because they are Jewish, their officiant wouldn't perform the ceremony until after sundown, which was somewhere around 9 p.m. No worries, we told them. So the evening started with the cocktail party, which was the most appropriate way to begin this extremely enjoyable affair.

DRINKS, DINNER,
DANCING & I DOS

Cindy & Ian

INVITE YOU TO
JOIN THEM FOR
THEIR WEDDING

NOT BLACK TIE

SATURDAY, JUNE 25, 2
THE WESTSIDE LOFT • 336 W
NEW YORK CI

KINDLY
REPLY

CINDY & IAN

BEFORE
JUNE 1st

YOUR NAME(S) HERE _____

WILL BE THERE WITH BELLS ON
☐ Friday (for cocktails)
☐ Saturday (for the wedding)
☐ Sunday (for lunch)

WOULD LOVE TO BE THERE BUT
☐ some of us work for a living
☐ don't really think it will last
☐ too upset Ian/Cindy is going off the market
☐ don't have enough weight watchers points
☐ other, please explain: _____

YOU'RE INVITED...

RESERVING A BLOCK
OF HOTEL ROOMS?
WHAT TO ASK.

1. What is the room rate for guests arriving a day or two early or staying late?

2. Exactly which rooms are being held for your guests? Not all rooms in a given hotel are the same. Ask about class of room, views, floor, size of beds, and how recently the rooms were renovated.

3. What happens if you don't fill the rooms or if you need more?

4. If you are reserving many rooms, will they give a discount on a suite for you?

5. Is the group rate lower than the discounted rates you are finding online? If it is, it is usually only for a limited number of rooms—but don't hesitate to grab them.

Your invitations set the tone of what's to come. In Cindy and Ian's case, they wanted it made clear that their wedding would be fun and informal. Inspired by Cindy's love of vintage French posters, we created a colorful printed card that was an illustration of a couple dancing on a rooftop with bubbles rising from their champagne. The wording was a cheerful declaration of their nuptials, and clearly printed at the bottom were the words "Not Black Tie." We also included the rehearsal dinner invitation as well as a Sunday brunch invite, which encouraged guests to "Bike it. Cab it. Drag yourself out of bed." The addresses were printed on labels that mimicked a vintage marquee (as did many of their subsequent paper products). The casual yet elegant mailing package was very much in the spirit of the upcoming event, accomplishing exactly what an invitation should.

HAVE A GOOD TIME

DOUBLE THE FUN

Cindy and Ian arranged for family members, friends, and the bridal party to stay at a particular hotel. How did they get this sizable crowd to their wedding venue across town? Easy: a double-decker bus. This is another example of making sure the entire experience is an enjoyable ride, literally and figuratively. Limousines are not the only transportation in town. Be creative and see what you come up with!

CREATE YOUR OWN DRESS CODE

Many couples assume they have to look like some version of the couple atop a wedding cake. Far from it. This wedding was nothing if not spontaneous in attitude and atmosphere, so why would the dress code be any different? Note some of their spirited touches.

~ The bride wore an olive-green dress just because she "liked the color."

~ The groom wore a graphic black-and-white paisley Paul Smith suit.

~ The bridesmaids wore colorful orchid wrist corsages on long silk ribbons à la *Sex and the City.*

~ The groom brought kneepads and a change of pants, so that at the end of the couple's first dance (a tango to Cake's version of "Perhaps, Perhaps, Perhaps") he could slide across the room on his knees. His pants ripped and were replaced soon after.

THE FRENCH BISTRO EFFECT

Imagine being able to create your ideal restaurant for an evening. There's no reason you can't approach your wedding dinner this way. Cindy and Ian rented a loft, which meant they could choose their caterer and rentals. Why not create a distinctive look, rather than generic wedding fare? In keeping with our French inspiration, we went for a bistro atmosphere, only with four long tables of forty people. To soften the industrial ceilings, we filled them with almost a hundred natural-paper lanterns in varying sizes, which added texture and ambiance.

GREAT CATERING IS ALL IN THE DETAILS. POINTS TO DISCUSS BEFORE COMMITTING

1. SERVICE
Be sure you have enough waiters in your contract to ensure smooth service. Ask your caterer the time it will take to serve each course, from the first to the last guest. Ideally, it should be under 10 minutes. If it is 15 minutes or more, ask how to bring this number down. Bottlenecks can come from an inadequate number of waiters or kitchen staff.

2. COCKTAIL HOUR
How many people are passing hors d'oeuvres? How many bartenders are there? When guests first arrive, waiters should pass drinks to everyone to alleviate pressure on the bar. Once guests have their drinks, switch to food. Are all of your guests getting food or is it only the people near the kitchen door? Make sure the waitstaff works the room.

3. ADDITIONAL COSTS
What are they charging for children? What age constitutes a child? How about vendor meal charges?

4. BAR
Check out what your caterer means by "full bar." You should be able to see a list of all the brands of liquor that will be offered. Will wine and champagne be passed at the bar during cocktails as well as served with dinner? Make sure you define it.

5. TEST IT
A tasting is the only way to ensure that the food served at your wedding is delicious and beautifully presented. Before signing a contract make sure one is included, and use this meeting to collaborate with your caterer to infuse the menu with your favorite foods and drinks.

The guests really enjoyed the intimacy of the large dining tables. We filled the ceiling with the natural paper lanterns and kept our dinner table decor very simple, yet chic.

THE ART OF TABLESCAPING

I call the process of designing tables "tablescaping" because, for me, it is very similar to landscaping. The canvas is a tabletop instead of an outdoor space. And just as landscaping isn't about a single tree or flower bed, tablescaping is not just about a centerpiece, but about designing with a myriad of tools. The elements include the flowers, the containers they are arranged in, tablecloths, china, stemware, silver, and candles. That said, you should never constrain your imagination. Just as with landscaping, sometimes it's the whimsical or unexpected touch that makes a tablescape truly exceptional. Always embrace the possibilities.

Given the chic, relaxed attitude of Cindy and Ian's wedding, the tablescape had to follow suit. Since it was a summer fete, whimsical touches like rattan chargers (platters) and bamboo silverware set the tone. Wide, ginger-colored silk runners with black grosgrain trim on the natural canvas linen punctuated the table. Accents included chunky square candles and bouquets of horsetails, mango-colored mini calla lilies, orchids, and peonies—all in modern square zinc containers. It was an unconventional table for sure, but it was a very distinctive one. Every element you add to the table—stemware, silverware, china—has to speak to the entire picture. If you're at a hotel or restaurant, by all means try to use as many of the venue's items as you can (they come with the price of the space), but always remember you can supplement with great rentals where needed. Don't worry about doing it all; go for the impact. A colored goblet and quirky silverware can transform an otherwise drab setting.

BEYOND FLOWERS

TABLE DECORATIONS

Important as they are, remember that flowers are just one element in decorating a table. If you were having a dinner party at home, would you rely only on flowers? Probably not. Whether as supplements or as alternatives, here are some suggestions that go beyond the usual suspects. Remember, everything on the table is part of the décor, down to the salt and pepper shakers you choose.

CANDLES

I really love candles. Selection and positioning can make such a huge statement, whether you go with tall, slender tapers, dramatic candelabras, modern square pillars, or a trail of votives. Remember, candles come in all different shapes, sizes, colors, and containers, so experiment and have some fun. Just make sure they are not scented.

FRUIT AND HERBS

Is there anything more alluring than a bowl of lemons, a goblet of champagne grapes, a cornucopia of lady apples, or fresh herbs tied with natural twine?

PLANTS

I love the look of plants—great palm trees, ming aralias, or hedges. Either buy them and use them later, or ask a wholesaler if it will rent them to you. I once used palm trees to help create a 50s Havana supper club feel.

MIRRORS

As with runners, mirrors look great and reflect the flowers or candles that are placed on them. You can glam things up with mirrors, either covering the entire top of the table or bar or just as a runner. You can use Plexiglas or antiqued mirrors, which are more expensive. You can find mirrors at any glass store and have them measured and cut for you.

MOCK IT UP

Don't wait for your wedding day to see if your table décor works. Mock it up in advance. I do it for all my clients and, invariably, many adjustments are made in the process. A table mock-up is where you literally gather the correct-sized tables, flowers, vases/containers, linens, settings, and so forth to do a dry run. This minimizes the likelihood of any surprises on your wedding day and gives you the opportunity to make improvements. I suggest doing it 1 to 6 weeks before the wedding so that your flowers are in season. Most vendors will rent (or even loan) your selected pieces to you for a day. If you can mock up a table at your venue, great, but many florists ask that it be in their shop. A mock-up is equivalent to a writer reviewing her work before handing it in. The difference is in the edits, fixes, and last-minute adjustments. You simply can't wait until the day of the event to see how your tables will look and feel. I know, it seems like a big pain—but you'll thank me for this one.

LEFT: *A rattan changer, bamboo silverware, and an orchid as a napkin treat create and finish this summery fête.* MIDDLE: *Rich ruby-red pillows and flowers for the dance party.* RIGHT: *Large bowls of floating candles and jewel-colored dahlias and roses.*

EVERYTHING IS SUBJECT TO CHANGE

Weddings are an organic process, with many variables happening all at once. The best of plans can go awry due to a change in weather, unforeseen complications, and last-minute circumstances. You simply can't control or predict how the day will unfold. So not only should you plan your wedding down to the last detail; you then need to be ready to scrap any one of them, should you sense something isn't working. Here are some examples.

IF TIMING GETS THROWN OFF, NOTIFY ALL WHO NEED TO KNOW

Cindy and Ian wrote their own vows—something I always love. What we didn't anticipate was that Cindy, being a wonderful writer, had a lot to say. That pushed back the dinner schedule, which normally wouldn't be a problem. But due to house rules, this wedding had to end by 1 A.M. Each slight delay would cut into the dance party later in the evening. The minute we sensed a shift in schedule, we immediately notified the kitchen staff, who re-timed their prep and service to help us make up time during the dinner without it feeling rushed.

READ THE CROWD AND BE READY TO ADAPT TO THEIR NEEDS

Cindy and Ian had a terrific DJ. Though she had a program of music that was created with Cindy and Ian, she noticed that the crowd went wild for a particular request by Ian. Sensing the crowd's reaction, she switched directions and went into a Southern Rock/80s Rock and Roll set, which kept everyone on the dance floor for a straight hour. This is an example of why you should look for professionals who know when and how to adjust to the uniqueness of your crowd.

YOU CAN'T MAKE PEOPLE DANCE

If you planned for a night of dancing but the dance floor is empty, you can do one of two things: try other kinds of music and do your personal best to get friends up. If that doesn't work, then accept that it may not be a dancing crowd and that you need to mellow it down and create a more loungey feel. Don't force energy where it doesn't want to be. Each crowd has its own personality; fighting it will only hurt your party.

DON'T INTERRUPT A FULL DANCE FLOOR

Conversely, if you have a crowd who are up on their feet, don't force them down! Go with the flow, even if it means postponing planned toasts or the cake-cutting ritual. You want your guests to enjoy themselves.

PLAN EVERY DETAIL AND PREPARE FOR EACH STEP BUT BE READY TO SHIFT GEARS AT ANY POINT.

SAY CHEESE

Ian is a true cheese connoisseur. In the spirit of sharing his passion with his guests, Ian set up a cheese table and had a cheese advisor to help people select something to their liking and pair it with the proper port. Not surprisingly, Ian himself also manned the table, enthusiastically making recommendations that complemented particular wines. If you love something, your passion will be infectious. What is more wonderful than sharing your true passion with everyone you love, especially on your wedding day?

A CAKE OF A DIFFERENT COLOR

There is no rule that says a wedding cake has to be white. If you love chocolate frosting, and most people do, by all means consider a chocolate-frosted cake—or any other kind of cake you desire. It's your cake: have it and eat it, too! Cindy and Ian's cake was inspired by an illustration. The white dots just happened to echo the white paper lanterns, which worked out great.

GIFTS FROM THE HEART

Gifts come in many forms, and Cindy and Ian received a few terrific ones. First, a good friend devised a cocktail in their honor, aptly named the Sin D'Ian Martini, which was served at the bar. The others were gifts of songs—two musical acts performed for the couple. One friend composed an original song in celebration of this very special day.

ON A PERSONAL NOTE

I love all the weddings we work on. But I have to say this was a real standout because in every way it was so "Cindy and Ian." Everything they did, every element they chose, reflected who they were as a couple, which made all the difference.

CELEBRATE WITH COCKTAILS

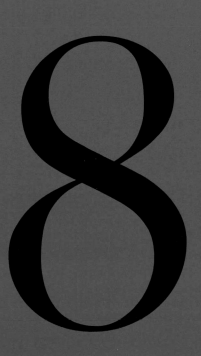

*Communal black Parsons tables with
metal stools are grouped so it feels like
a high-energy restaurant.*

Lately, we've been getting requests for cocktail party–style weddings. And why not? In theory, they sound wonderful: light and breezy, lots of music and dancing, great passed food, and your guests won't feel stuck at one table for the night. Aren't cocktails the best part of a wedding anyway? Maybe you'll even save some money. We'd all like to either host or attend such an affair. That's in theory, of course. In actuality, it's not easy to pull off a cocktail wedding—and trust me, it's not necessarily cheaper either. Venues have revenue minimums, and whatever style of reception you hold, it will still require food, music, décor, and paper products. Yet the biggest issue to contend with is structure.

How do you create an interesting party where people won't leave after one hour? There's a reason for the term "cocktail hour." You drink, you chat, you leave. Your wedding should be treated as the monumental event it is and not something guests flit in and out of at whim.

But you can well achieve the free-wheeling *spirit* of a cocktail party. You just have to give it an almost invisible structure, one that keeps the energy high and momentum going for the five or so hours for which you've rented your venue. As with any successful event, it's all a matter of timing, creating various atmospheres, and having surprises along the way. You also have to anticipate your guests' needs and provide satisfying food and places to eat and lounge. No matter how much someone wants to share in your joy, they are not going to endure a night of standing. But they will adore a night of dancing, great food, and the freedom to move around in a room full of fun things to do and experience.

THE STORY OF

Lauren and Christopher

I love everything about second weddings. Usually the couple just wants to have a wonderful party, and you can really feel the love all around you. Lauren and Christopher's wedding was a great example. Now in their mid-30s, the two had managed to go to the same college and share many mutual friends without meeting each other—until years later, at a funeral. Lauren, an outgoing photographer, was divorced, and Christopher, a handsome optometrist, had no interest in marriage—until he met Lauren, that is. Given that Lauren's first wedding was a huge, formal affair, the two wanted theirs to be more of an elaborate cocktail party than a traditional wedding. To set the tone, they invited their 300 guests to a live music venue they took over the night before the wedding, where Chris was one of the "headliners." Everything about this wedding was enjoyable to work on, especially the creative and generous spirit with which the bridal couple approached their big day.

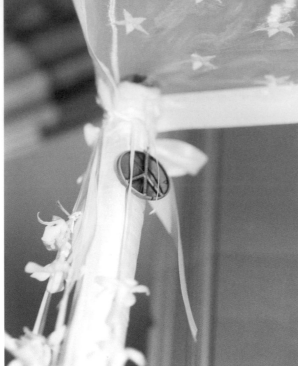

The chuppah, flanked by flowering dogwood branches, contained a very special detail.

A MOTHER'S TOUCH

Though this chapter is more about the party than the ceremony, I have to share a small but extraordinary touch. When Chris was a baby, his mother hung a metal peace symbol over his crib. After his mother died, the peace symbol became an emotional talisman for Chris. It also became the perfect way to include his mother's memory in the service. It hung in the chuppah and, given its importance, we guarded it with our lives after the ceremony. I love touches like this because they are small and private and therefore incredibly meaningful.

Initial floor plan: In this 5,000-square-foot space, we needed to accommodate a dining area with food, dance space, and lounge areas while making the space feel cohesive, fun, and energetic.

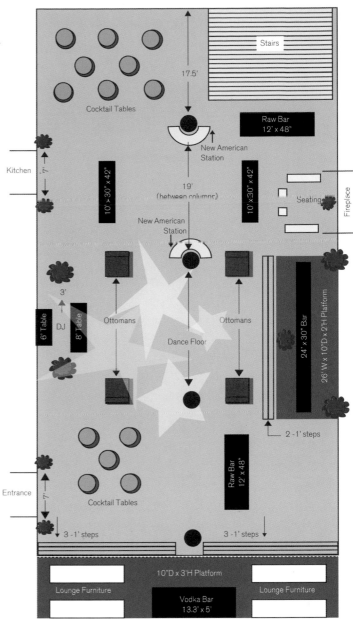

48'

Stairs

17.5'

Cocktail Tables

Raw Bar
12' x 48'

New American
Station

Kitchen

7'

10' x 30' x 42"

10' x 30' x 42"

Seating

Fireplace

19'
(between columns)

New American
Station

3'

6' Table   DJ   8' Table

Ottomans   Ottomans

Dance Floor

24' x 30' Bar

26' W x 10'D x 2'H Platform

2 - 1' steps

Cocktail Tables

Raw Bar
12' x 48'

Entrance

7'

3 - 1' steps   3 - 1' steps

10"D x 3'H Platform

Lounge Furniture   Lounge Furniture

Vodka Bar
13.3' x 5'

AN INTERESTING VENUE

For a cocktail-style wedding, I find it best to steer clear of traditional spaces. You really want a multifaceted venue, or one that gives you space to create. Remember, you need to fill the space with a bar, a lounge area, and a dance floor, as well as several places for people to wander into and sit down, for conversation or eating. We found a great place in Manhattan that had a modern art gallery in front, a charming former tea parlor, and a beautifully restored grand ballroom. Each space had its own character and proportion. Best of all, it was a not-for-profit space with a mission to save the homeless. The idea of giving back was especially important to Lauren, so we all were thrilled with the choice. The tea parlor with its latticework became the ceremony space. The modern gallery (which happened to have a cool exhibition going on) was the first reception area, for the cocktail hour before the cocktail wedding. Later, when we opened the space into the ballroom, we kept the doors open so guests could return at any point to the gallery and its access to the street.

A 24-foot-long bar says cocktail party to me! We had mirrored panels in the front custom built, along with tall black shelves behind the bar that held candles, glassware, and champagne bottles. Bamboo trees and papyrus greenery added some softer touches.

Vodka bar—served martinis and lemon-lime, watermelon, and pineapple-infused vodka.

ADDED INTEREST

As great as this space was, I knew we could improve on it. (Lesson: always push the envelope of creativity.) Here are some architectural elements we brought in.

~ In the gallery, a bar and a very modern-looking sushi counter were installed, as well as a portrait-photo booth.

~ In the ballroom, a specially built bar displayed a dramatic set of 12-foot shelves dotted with candles.

~ Also in the ballroom, we created an elevated section with platforms for lounging, which served to give the space more dimension. This provided an identifiable focal point.

~ The two center pillars were used to create the dance space; huge ottomans were placed in the four corners to further define the area.

~ A platform with a Lucite bar was built for the DJ, giving the room a logical point for toasts.

~ Several cozy seating nooks were created, one with café tables, another with sofas in front of the fireplace, and one with a vodka bar and loungers. Two long communal dining tables allowed guests to pull up a chair and socialize as they ate.

LOTS TO SEE, LOTS TO DO

As you can tell, there was a lot going on. The music was intentionally louder by the dance floor and softer in the seating areas. This way, if elderly relatives wanted to settle themselves in one place for the evening, they could. Food was both passed around and available at stations, so guests could decide how they wished to eat. The photo booth was open for pictures. And of course the dance floor was central to the entertainment.

Sushi station—very clean and simple design, covered in natural tatami.

A NOVEL TREAT

Lauren and Chris happened to love vodka. Why not take their passion and share it with their friends? We set up a vodka bar that had vodka infusions as well as a choice of several martinis. You could opt instead to do a chocolate bar or a cheese bar. The point is, it's a fun, unexpected experience that lets you share what you love with your guests.

A NIGHT OF STARRS

Chris's last name is Starr, a symbol too good not to take advantage of. Since Lauren was taking his name, we decided to make it the wedding's motif. As you would expect, stars appeared on the invitations, programs, and other paper goods. The top center of the ice sculpture was a beautifully faceted star that was lit from below. The cloth on the cake table was an embroidered organza overlay of differently sized and shaped stars. The theme was carried through on cupcakes, and linzer cookies were shaped, naturally, like stars! Perhaps the biggest hit of all was when we had stars put into the lighting system, so when Lauren and Chris danced their first dance, they literally were surrounded by stars, which, though stationary before their dance, started moving all around them.

CONSIDER THE EXTERIOR

A quick word about interesting places: they don't always have the most welcoming exteriors. This one was on an industrial street and the venue's entrance wasn't exactly grand. No matter—we hired some people to clean up the street and rented two 12-foot palm trees to flank the door. Parking cones marked the front so that taxis and parking valets could pull right up to the venue's door. Don't leave anything to chance. Your wedding shouldn't feel like a speakeasy. Arrivals and departures greatly matter. They make the first and last impressions.

MANAGING THE EVENING'S ENERGY AND FLOW

These rules of thumb hold true for any wedding but are especially important at a cocktail-style wedding, where the structure isn't as self-evident.

USE THE MUSIC'S TEMPO TO GUIDE THE MOOD AND MOMENT

Whenever you slow down or pump up the music, guests intuitively know what to do. You don't have to instruct them to get up or leave the dance floor. There are songs you simply can't dance to. At the cocktail party, the style of music and its tempo play an especially big role in staging the evening.

THE FIRST TOAST IS DESIGNED TO WELCOME GUESTS

Toasts play many roles. They welcome people, they precede dinner, or they can introduce a dance set. I strongly suggest the first toast not come from the bride and groom. Let your parents or the best man/maid of honor do the welcome toasts.

TIME TOASTS WISELY

Guests never finish eating a course at the same time. This creates an awkward period when nothing is happening and energy often plummets. Fill it with a toast or two and then transition into the next dance set. If you have more than two toasts, don't jam them together. It's boring to listen to a row of speeches, and it's better if you pepper them throughout the evening.

MAKE SURE YOUR DJ OR BAND LEADER IS IN SYNCH
WITH EITHER YOUR PLANNER OR MAÎTRE D'

This is critical. One hand must know what the other hand is doing to ensure organic transitions from dancing to dining and back. You don't want dead air before food service has begun. It's better to have the service begin during the last set of music so that it feels quicker, not slower, than called for.

GIVE YOUR TOAST AT THE SAME TIME AS THE CAKE CUTTING

This is a perfect opportunity to thank your guests and share whatever thoughts you would like. Know what you want to say and keep it less than 3 minutes. Your toast should lead into the final dance set which should be 30 to 45 minutes or so.

An intimate seating area is illuminated by square pillar candles on the mantle.

DON'T FORGET TO EAT!

You must remember to eat. Most brides and grooms are so busy dancing and socializing that they don't sit down long enough to eat the wonderful menu they helped create. (I can't tell you how many bridal couples wind up ordering room service afterward at their hotels.) You may want to ask the kitchen to pack up two dinners for you. How fun to go back to your room and privately relive your day as you nibble away on a meal of your own design.

BREAKFAST MENU

AS A SPECIAL THANK YOU,
WE ARE DELIVERING A BAG OF
BREAKFAST GOODS TO YOUR DOOR BY 8:30AM

YOUR BREAKFAST WILL INCLUDE:

✓ BUTTER CROISSANT
✓ STICKY BUN
✓ SCONE
✓ FRESH FRUIT AND BERRIES
✓ FRESH-SQUEEZED ORANGE JUICE
✓ NEW YORK TIMES

PLEASE FEEL FREE TO ORDER
COFFEE THROUGH ROOM SERVICE, ON US.

XO,
DR. AND MRS. STARR

FARINE
DE
FROMENT

Fabrication
Traditionnelle

BALTHAZAR

BOULANGERIE

CROISSANTS
& GATEAUX

80 Spring Street
· NEW YORK ·
phone: 965 1785

BREAKFAST MENU

As a special thank you,
we are delivering a bag of
breakfast goods to your door by 9:30AM

Your breakfast will include:

☑ Butter croissant
☑ Sticky bun
☑ Scone
☑ Fresh fruit and berries
☑ Fresh squeezed orange juice
☑ New York Times

Please feel free to order
coffee through room service, on us.

XO
Dr. and Mrs. Starr

MORNING-AFTER BREAKFAST TREAT

If many of your guests are staying at a hotel in which you booked the rooms, here's a thoughtful idea. Rather than organize a formal breakfast, have it sent to their rooms. We designed a personal "room service" menu and hung it on each guest's doorknob during the party. When guests returned to their rooms, they read that Lauren and Chris were having continental breakfast and the Sunday *Times* delivered to their doors by 9:30 A.M. This way, everyone got to sleep in, including the newlyweds.

GIVE TRADITION A HOME SPIN

I LOVE A MODERN WEDDING,

but I love a traditional approach every bit as much. The very act of marrying is a tradition, so there's great reason to embrace tried-and-true customs. Happily there is no one tradition, no one way to get married. Even if there were, you couldn't help but give it your own spin. Every bridal couple is unique and so are the circumstances behind their wedding. I urge you to use what's unique about you to personalize the day so it becomes truly yours and no one else's. We've all been to those forgettable weddings that blur into one another. That happens because the couple blindly agrees to everything the catering manager or florist suggests. (These providers have done these things a million times before and could do it all again in their sleep.) You could say you don't know any better—after all, you're not a wedding planner. But I would argue you have an opinion in every other aspect of your life, especially when it comes to any kind of sizable investment, such as a car or a home.

Now is not the time to go along to get along. Now is the time to question every element, every decision. It's the time to ask yourself if you could do something differently, if you could push the envelope, whether it's something as simple as the color and fabric of your table linens or as huge as eschewing a ballroom in favor of an outdoor setting.

THE STORY OF

Eliza and Joel

Eliza and Joel are a lovely, picture-perfect couple in their late 20s. Both film producers, they met on a shoot and are amazingly compatible. They came to us after things hadn't worked out with another planner. Many elements had already been decided. For example, they knew they wanted to have their wedding ceremony at a wonderfully charming local school church. They also wanted to have the reception at Eliza's family property, which happened to be part of the family-owned vineyard. The grounds were on top of a hill overlooking the vineyard; the views were vast and nothing short of spectacular. It was incredibly peaceful, and you felt as if you were in heaven. There was even an alley of trees that could be used as a drive-through entrance to the event. It would be hard to find a more beautiful location, especially for late June. The couple knew what kind of food and, of course, what kind of wine they wanted to serve. They also had a guest list of 250, many of whom would be attending the rehearsal dinner. Style-wise, the couple wanted a wedding with a romantic, turn-of-the-century look, while maintaining many traditional elements. At the same time, they stressed that they wanted the affair to be laid-back and unpretentious. The objective was to keep everything simple and play up the country charm while infusing just the right degree of elegance and sophistication.

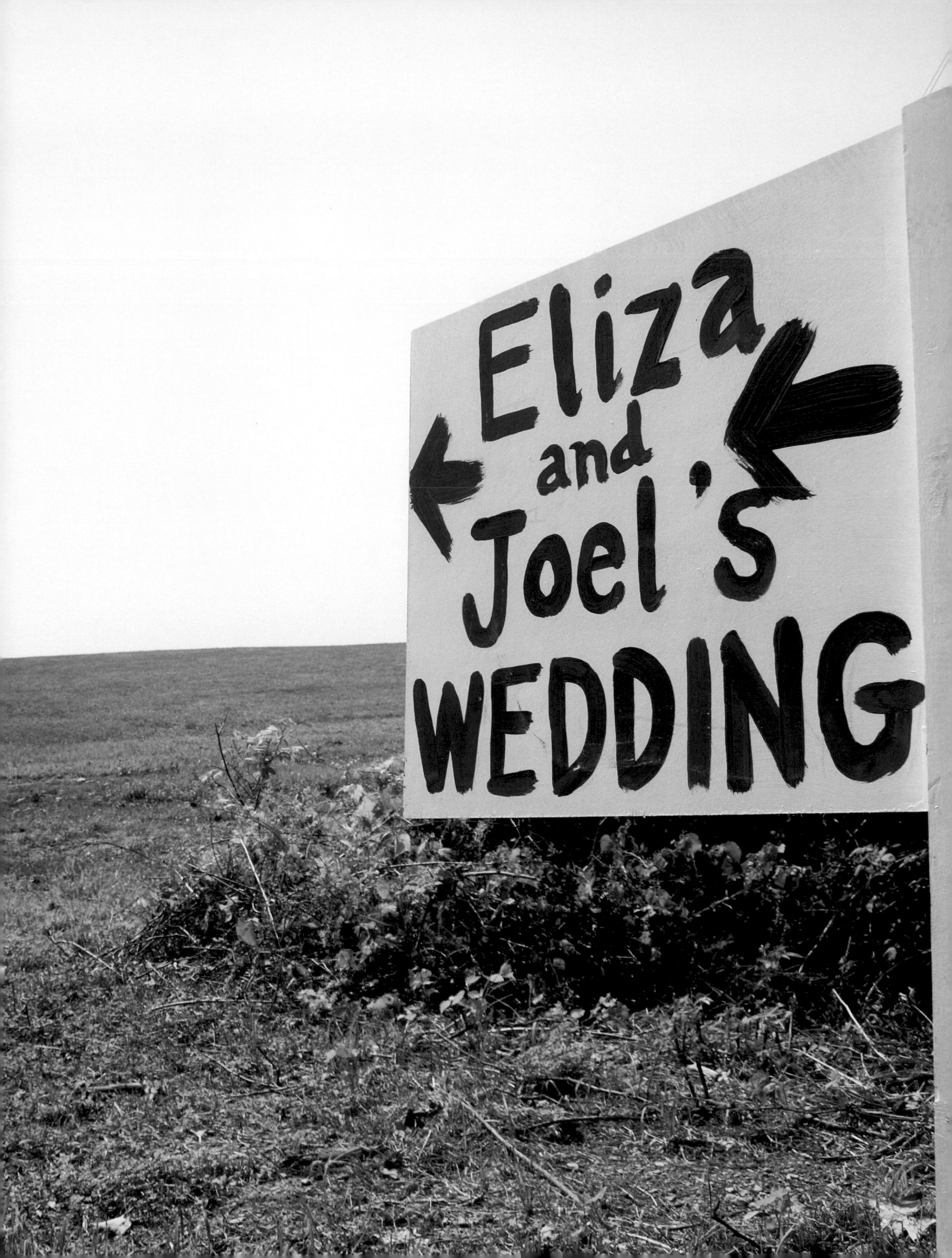
Eliza
and
Joel's
WEDDING

PLEASE JOIN US FOR A

⊸PIG ROAST⊸

IN HONOR OF

ELIZA AND JOEL

FRIDAY, JUNE 24TH

5:00 PM

MAPLE TOR FARM

37 WING ROAD

MILLBROOK, NEW YORK

———

SUSAN AND PETER LEVANGIA

KINDLY REPLY TO SUSAN
845.555.1416 OR LEVANGIA@ATT.NET

The Friday night rehearsal dinner was a pig roast. The pig was the motif for the invitation.

THE REHEARSAL DINNER ISN'T REALLY A REHEARSAL

This may seem obvious, but you'd be surprised how many couples think the dinner has to relate to the wedding, at least thematically. It doesn't. Moreover, I would say it shouldn't. The rehearsal dinner can have a completely different ambiance, reflecting yet another side to your personalities. Why take away from the impact of the wedding in any way? Eliza and Joel had a pig roast for their rehearsal dinner. A pig motif appeared on the invitation as well as on a giant escort sign (with seating chart serendipitously pinned to it). The table centerpieces were a variety of potted flowers in mossy terra-cotta urns. Wine bottles were on a rustic table created with a butcher block top and dish towels offered as dinner napkins. We filled wine barrels with ice and old-fashioned bottles of soda. A bottle opener was tied to the barrel with twine. All of this added to the great casual charm. Dinner was a buffet-style barbecue. Everything had a down-home feel, which couldn't have been further from the country elegance of the next day.

Previous chapters cover choosing your venue, be it a public space, a loft, a ballroom, or the outdoors. Once that decision is made, you probably have a good overall idea of the style you're going for. You're ready to fine-tune. Start flipping through magazines—not just bridal, but every kind you can get your hands on: home design, garden, fashion, and so forth—as well as catalogs and travel and resort brochures. Cut out anything you like. There could be a beautiful cosmetic ad with a color you love, an inspiration from a resort or posh hotel ad—whatever moves you. An aesthetic will start to emerge. If you're drawn to old-fashioned drawing rooms or clean, modern lines, you'll know it. Not only will this collage help you find your direction, it will help you communicate your look to your vendors, starting with the florist. It will show them the kind of style, textures, and colors you love—a visual calling card, bridging the gap between descriptive words and actually showing people what you want.

A TENT WITH A VIEW

You couldn't look at Eliza's family property without wanting to take advantage of its views. We timed the wedding so that during cocktails the guests could enjoy a majestic sunset. A round open-air tent faced the vineyard's valley. To direct the eye outside rather than in, a large-scale bar was constructed around the tent's center pole. The burnt-orange raw silk used for the bar linens perfectly complemented the sunset. The views were truly remarkable, so I changed the floor plan at the last minute—you have to be flexible and allow for change when need be. The bar was as dramatic as it was functional while people milled about admiring the breathtaking sunset.

TRUE ROMANCE

Because Eliza and Joel loved the idea of creating a turn-of-the-century feel, décor was important. We set about making everything look like it was brought outside from an estate's pantry. Colors were sumptuous and textures luxurious, yet nothing looked forced or designed to impress.

FOR THE CHURCH

A lush, 40-foot green garland accented with white hung over the church's main entrance. This told both guests and passers-by that something wonderful was happening inside.

Instead of the typical two floral arrangements at the altar, we opted for a single giant one in a rusty, cast-iron urn. The pews had sisal cones filled with a variety of ferns. Because the church was so white, using greens made it warm and inviting.

FOR THE DINNER TENT

The tables and chairs made a great contribution to the country feel. The crisp metal bistro chairs used during the cocktail hour were also practical as they did not dig into the lawn. Inexpensive metal cocktail tables were purchased so the legs could be exposed, displaying the crisp points of the hem-stitched linen. (With most rental tables, cloths need to go to the floor to cover the unsightly legs.)

~ The tabletops looked like eighteenth-century still-lifes. The floral arrangements were lush and effortless to enhance their inherent grace.

~ We used an eclectic array of charming flower vessels, from vintage teapots to footed tarnished-silver bowls.

~ Place settings featured mix-and-match fine floral-patterned china.

~ The water tumblers were slightly fluted with an old-fashioned quality. Grape leaves acted as coasters.

~ The table setting included bottles of olive oil to foster the old-country look.

~ The dance floor was lit with sunset-colored, oversized silk lampshades.

LEFT: *A pair of wreaths and lush garlands frame the chapel doors to make it inviting.* ABOVE: *Simple cones filled with ferns for the pew markers; single lush greenery for the altar arrangement. I like the asymmetry.*

THE GREAT NAPKIN DEBATE

Eliza and Joel's napkins were an important element of the table setting. They were quality hem-stitched linen, and after the wedding Eliza's mother had them cleaned and sent to their guests as a gift—a unique and thoughtful gesture I just loved. It won't surprise you to hear I'm a bit of a stickler about napkins. I don't like unusual napkin folds, including the latest trend for origami. A napkin should not look like a fan, a cook's cap, a boat, or any other nonsense, unless, of course, it is for a children's party. I believe in functionality. I know sometimes people rent decorative napkins that are silk or embroidered with beading. At the end of the day, napkins are for wiping, usually your mouth, so they should feel nice and do what they are supposed to. To me, nothing beats a great cotton or linen napkin. You can rent them, but you can also buy them in bulk. If a discount store near you is having a sale, consider buying a neutral color that will work with any palette. I recently bought a large batch of beautiful hem-stitched napkins at a closeout sale at Williams Sonoma for less than $3 a napkin.

THE ENVELOPE PLEASE
Consider folding the napkin like an envelope and placing it on the plate with a menu card tucked into the fold.

MR. AND MRS. JOHN STUART DYSON

REQUEST THE HONOUR OF YOUR PRESENCE

AT THE MARRIAGE OF THEIR DAUGHTER

ELIZA MACGREGOR

TO

MR. JOEL MICHAEL LEVANGIA

SATURDAY, THE TWENTY-FIFTH OF JUNE

TWO THOUSAND AND FIVE

AT HALF AFTER FIVE O'CLOCK

FLAGLER MEMORIAL CHAPEL

MILLBROOK, NEW YORK

DIRECTIONS

THE FAVOUR OF A REPLY IS REQUESTED BY

THE TWENTY-FIFTH OF MAY

RECEPTION TO FOLLOW

IMMEDIATELY AFTER THE CEREMONY

THE HILL ABOVE THE VINEYARDS

677 BANGALL ROAD

MILLBROOK, NEW YORK

PAPER PERFECT

Every wedding starts with paper products. The invitation sets the tone for what's to come. It is the first impression your guests will have of your wedding. As previously discussed, save-the-date cards can (and should) stand on their own. They should be eye-catching, serendipitous cards that tell people to mark their calendars. But what about the invitation, RSVP card, menu card, and wedding program? Where do you start to create your look? Though it can be an expensive proposition, my suggestion is first to consider quality and service. You want to work with someone who will not only walk you through your options, but will test-sample and proof the final product. If you cut corners to save money, you could wind up with a poorly executed product you wouldn't dare send out. *Do not shortchange this important category!* Go for the best stock you can afford. If it means sticking to a simpler design, so be it. Better to have classic, elegant fonts on a high-grade paper than all sorts of bells, whistles, and bows on paper that's barely a cut above copy paper. Note the following paper pointers.

Very classic and elegant invitation set. We designed a Victorian pattern that was letterpressed on the back of the invitation as well as the liner. We also pulled a decorative ornament from the liner and blew it up for the reception card and directions booklet.

COORDINATE, DON'T MATCH YOUR PAPERS

For Eliza and Joel's wedding, we used a vintage wallpaper pattern for the envelope liner, the back of the invitation, and the reception cards. A motif from this pattern appeared on the cover of their programs and again on their thank-you note cards. The menu card design border was altogether different, but still in the same spirit. This design repetition really brands your wedding as something distinctive and unique.

HEAVY STOCK HAS ITS ADVANTAGES

Not only does it look and feel important, but envelopes made from heavy stock require the recipient to open them in the traditional way and experience the full impact of the lining. Lightweight paper envelopes, conversely, invite slitting with a letter opener, leaving the liner unnoticed and unappreciated. With heavy stock there is no need to do an inner and outer envelope, where the outer is sealed and the inner is the beautiful one. This practice harkens back to the days when the letter carriers brought mail by horse. The outer envelope was usually soiled from the travel and would be discarded. However charming that sounds, it's an unnecessary waste of paper in today's world.

THERMOGRAPHY IS NOT ENGRAVING

I wish I could tell you to save a bundle and go with thermography instead of engraving. But there's a huge difference between the two. Things usually cost more for a reason. For engraving, metal plates need to be made; it is an old-fashioned way of printing. Thermography is a modern-day invention, where powder is mixed into the ink and when it dries, it creates the raised effect on the paper. That may be fine with you, but be aware of the distinction so you're not disappointed later.

SEND BLANK RSVP CARDS

I'm not a fan of check-off boxes. In this regard, I am old-fashioned. Traditionally, when someone received an invitation, they would reply with a written note on their personal stationery. People don't do this anymore, so we provide them with the card, the envelope, and even a postage stamp. But I think it's nice to give your guests a blank card so they may write you a personal note. To be extra careful, number the RSVP cards to correspond to your guest list. If a person forgets to sign his or her name (this happens more often than you'd think), you'll have a way to identify the writer.

LEAVE ROOM FOR PERSONALIZATION ON MENU CARDS

I usually opt for a clean, no-clutter look, which is why I like to use the menu card as the place card, too. Leave space on the menu card so you can use calligraphy for the guest's name. Hence, one piece of paper on a plate. And please, please do a seating chart. Again, it's my old-fashioned side at work. Your guests will feel so special when they are not just directed to a table but to a particular seat, where you think they may enjoy sitting next to so-and-so and across from so-and-so.

INSIST ON SEEING THE TEST PAPERS

Even if you're working with someone you trust, you'd be amazed at the variations in paper once it has been processed. Everything from the ink and paper color, to the cut of the card should be seen and approved by you. Better to be unhappy with a test than boxes and boxes of the finished (and paid for) final product. Get a sample proof from your calligrapher too. The ink color, style, and how it will fill up the envelope matter. Look at an addressed card with the chosen stamp to make sure it all goes together perfectly.

THE POWER OF THE WEDDING BAND

Some of the best parties incorporate both a band and a DJ. In the case of Eliza and Joel, their band had booked another job before the wedding. The other event was a good two hours away. Once I learned of this, I was nervous. Too much was at stake for us to consider the possibility of the band showing up late due to traffic. Music is so important in setting the tone and creating the mood. I wanted to open up the dinner tent and have the band play classic standards to really make the event timeless. The best way to achieve this, especially early on, is to do it with live musicians so the party can harness its energy. To be safe, we hired a great DJ, too. The band showed up on time and played the first set. We coordinated the band and the DJ, which made for an awesome party because we got the greatest range of music. This played to the band's strength, which was more rock and contemporary, and allowed the DJ to kick in with the other styles.

There aren't words to express just how important the right wedding talent is, be it a DJ or a band. Next to the ceremony (and the couple, of course), the music is the star attraction. Music can unite or divide the generations; it controls the energy flow and determines whether people are happy on the dance floor or are out in the hallways trying to catch a break from the ear-pounding noise.

For some reason, many bandleaders and DJs feel a need to talk incessantly throughout the evening. You want to work with someone who won't make it all about himself and who knows how to read and adapt song and genre selection to the crowd reaction. I've seen everything from awe-inspiring bands to those who have single-handedly ruined an affair. The only surefire way to get it right is to hire someone who enhanced a wedding you enjoyed. Short of that, here are some things to look and ask for when interviewing bands or DJs.

STICK WITH MUSIC TALENT WHO HAVE PLAYED AT PRIVATE SOCIAL EVENTS

Performing at weddings is a very different experience from a club or a concert. The needs are specific and diverse and this isn't the time for on-the-job training. The more experience, the better. For weddings, you want to work with talent who understand how to get all age groups onto the dance floor early in the evening. If you lose guests at the start of the evening, it is hard to win them back. Also, your music talent must have the ability to respond to the audience at hand, watch how the crowd reacts to each song, and switch tempos if need be. The power of an experienced bandleader is enormous.

REQUIRE THE BAND TO HAVE AT LEAST TWO VOCALISTS— ONE MALE, ONE FEMALE

There's simply no way one vocalist can carry an evening, let alone make every song sound different. Make sure you know the names of the vocalists and that you are getting the talent you listened to for your wedding.

INSIST ON GENRE DIVERSITY AND A GOOD MIX OF FAST AND SLOW

Although you may only love one type of music, dancing to one genre will get old after awhile. Make sure that your band or DJ understands how to play different genres well.

KNOW THE IMPORTANCE OF A SMOOTH FLOW

There are three essential elements the band needs to allow for great flow at a wedding. First, the music talent should be able to move from one song to the next without a pause. Second, the music should be continuous throughout the evening. If the band needs to take a break during dinner, they should leave one or two musicians on stage to play background music. If they will not do this, opt to play a CD with music you have preselected. Finally, your music talent should only speak when you ask him or her to speak. A good music director understands how to let music selection guide the evening; guests won't need to be told artificially when to stand up, sit down, or applaud.

ASK THE OBVIOUS

Are you the band's only commitment for the evening? When do they plan to set up and do sound checks? You don't want them dragging their equipment through your cocktail service, nor do you want to hear strange testing noises in the next room.

NO ADVERTISING

Some bands like to advertise themselves by passing out cards, putting their names on their drums or band stands, and the like. Nix any and all marketing attempts. If people like them, they will ask you for their number. Your flowers don't have the florist's name written on the vase and your caterer does not wear a shirt with the company's logo. For a band to do it is the same thing—tacky!

COUNTRY COMFORT

Always think of your guests' comfort. Try to anticipate any problems, issues, or concerns. For a country wedding, have water trucks spray the dirt roads to pack them down and avoid dust. Spray the area for fleas and ticks and provide bug spray in the lavatories, should guests want to spray their ankles. Next to the trailers, you may want big old comfy wicker chairs set up like a lounge to give it a homey feeling, should someone want to sit down and stay awhile. Although for Natalia and Todd the setting was in the country, their wedding was elegant and gracious. All the guests were incredibly well taken care of. There were extra town cars available at the end of the night for the guests who could not drive, and parking valets made it very convenient for the guests, especially in the dark country setting. Shuttle buses ran often to hotels, so guests did not have to wait if they wanted to leave early. Because the party was so much fun, no one left until the very, very end—a sign of a truly wonderful affair.

FORGET-ME-NOTS

10

NOT ONE OF THE WEDDINGS YOU'VE JUST ATTENDED IN THIS BOOK EVEN REMOTELY RESEMBLED ANOTHER. THE REASON IS SIMPLE: THE COUPLES DIDN'T REMOTELY RESEMBLE ONE ANOTHER.

Each couple brought to the table their own personalities, families, and circumstances. In every case, my job was to help them create a wedding that would speak to that unique equation.

Creativity comes from looking within and thinking about who you are and what you love most in life. Originality is not pulled out of a hat or a menu of sensational concepts. It comes from you and you alone. The last thing I want is for you to duplicate any of the weddings in this book. Rather, walk away inspired to create something wholly your own.

The biggest trend in the wedding industry today is personalizing your wedding. Unfortunately, incorporating unusual and trendy ideas into your wedding is very different from personalizing it. I can't think of anything more impersonal than utilizing a bunch of ideas that you read about in a magazine. Think of all the weddings you've been to. Which was your favorite? What do you remember most about it? I'm guessing it was a wedding that felt like a great dinner party and made you feel included in a very special event in someone's life. No doubt there was a feeling of warmth and goodwill throughout the room. You learned something about the couple, their culture, their families and friends. Maybe the food was wonderful. Maybe the room was gloriously designed. But the standouts were the energy and the hospitality—mixing with other guests, music, the dancing, and being well cared for.

Now think of one of your least favorite weddings. You were probably stuck at a table with people you had nothing in common with. The music pounded in your ears. Service took forever. Most of all, the night felt soulless and generic. Been there, done that; you were just glad when the cake was cut because you felt you could leave without being rude. Unfortunately, we've all been to that kind of wedding.

In a way, you want to plan a wedding backward, meaning you start with the end in mind. What would you most like to look back on? Did everyone feel included and special? Did they have a good time? Did you have a good time? Did your families come together in a meaningful and respectful way? Did you share your passions? Did the décor reflect your taste as a couple? Did your guests never want to leave? At the end of the day, what will matter most? What will stick in your and your guests' memories? You enjoyed every minute of the evening; it felt seamless.

Great memories aren't an accident. They're the result of careful planning and consideration. It's only in the planning stages that you have the power to ensure a truly unforgettable wedding.

THE THOUGHT THAT COUNTS

It is goodwill shown through hospitality that fosters exuberant energy from all of your guests. It is one of the few things that doesn't depend on money or budget—it is about intent. This is something that is priceless and doesn't cost much of anything to create.

THE MELTING POT THEORY
Most weddings are multigenerational, including your grandparents, your parents' friends, and, of course, your own friends. Even if you listen to hip-hop 24/7, you don't want to hire a hip-hop band in the name of "this is who we are." Your grandparents will scream. (Suggestion: older people retire early—hold the Snoop Dogg until later in the evening.) You have to think about every detail from your guests' perspective and strike a balance.

OLDER PEOPLE
Where are they sitting? Is it convenient and near the dance floor so they feel a part of things even if they remain seated the whole night? Have you located them far enough from the speakers so that the music won't be too loud? Can you play any songs that will get them onto the dance floor? Have you honored them by reference or by a thank-you in your speech?

PARENTS
Have you conferred with them on details? Have you reviewed the seating chart with them, especially where their friends are concerned? Most important, remember to thank them after the wedding. A heartfelt handwritten note (no emails!) or a dinner—just the four or six of you (in-laws, too)—will go a long way in showing your appreciation.

YOUNG PARENTS
Are their kids invited? Do you want to set up a room with babysitters where guests can leave their children during the wedding? Or do you simply provide them with numbers of babysitters or a service that they can use to leave their kids at home?

SINGLE FRIENDS
Have you thought about matchmaking possibilities in the seating arrangement? Do you need to keep an old boyfriend/girlfriend at separate tables?

IT'S THE
LITTLE THINGS

There's a reason why a phrase sticks: it's universal and true. If you do nothing else, stop and think about your guests' comfort from the minute they arrive to the minute they leave. If someone is uncomfortable, they cannot have a good time.

HOTEL ACCOMMODATIONS
Do your guests have a convenient and affordable place to stay? Don't make them scramble; offer them alternatives or block some rooms to get a reduced rate from your local hotel.

TRANSPORTATION
We've shown you various situations where help is needed. Church-to-venue transfers, valet parking, umbrellas to keep everyone dry, shawls to keep them warm—whatever it takes, do it!

COAT CHECK
Is it convenient or will it entail waiting in a long line? You can always hire an extra attendant or two depending on the number of guests you have.

CATFRING/MENU
Is there enough to eat? Is there enough selection for vegetarians or those with allergies and food restrictions? If you have very young guests, what will they eat? Is the service attentive and fast? Is the food hot? If it is a buffet and there are more than one hundred people, consider mirroring or duplicating the buffet, so there are no long lines. Food lines definitely do not connote elegant affair.

SEATING
Have you figuratively put yourself in each guest's seat? Is it a place that would lend good conversation with people other than just those on either side? Do they have a lot in common with those around them?

COMFORT
Is the room too dark or too light? Too loud, too hot, or too cold? Are your guests comfortable?

PARTING GIFTS
No, I don't necessarily mean favors. I mean what will their last impression be? Will it be struggling to hail a cab or find their car in the dark? Or will it be hot chocolate, or perhaps a takeaway muffin for breakfast with a note of thanks tucked in, as a valet brings their car around?

You can't do it all, but you can certainly do what matters most. Anything that makes a lasting impression is worth the effort. If it makes a guest feel welcome and valued, it is worth the sacrifice in other areas. Without question, this is your big day. Everyone is there to wish you well and share in your happiness. The more you give of yourself, the more goodwill you will receive, and the better the foundation you'll build to start your marriage. A wedding is the beginning of your personal history as a family.

I wish you a wedding you and your guests will never forget.

CREDITS

INTRODUCTION
Photographs on pages 14 and 18–19 by Christian Oth

CHAPTER 1
Photographs by Christian Oth
Save-the-Date created by Trevor Hoey
Drawing on page 43 by Ella Kruglyanskaya
Florist: Fête
Location: Sonnenalp Resort of Vail

CHAPTER 2
Photos by Jeremy Saladyga, Gruber Photographers New York
Cake by Sylvia Weinstock Cakes, Ltd.
Paper Products: Design Dairy
Florist: LMD Floral Events Interiors
Location: Peter White Studios

CHAPTER 3
All photographs by Christian Oth, except pages 31, 43, and 86, which are by Garrett Holden
Cake by Sylvia Weinstock Cakes, Ltd.
Save-the-Dates, menu cards, and wedding programs: Russell Sloane
Florist: LMD Floral Events Interiors
Location: Cipriani 42nd Street
Calligraphy: Marian Rodenhizer

CHAPTER 4
Photographs by Philippe Cheng
Cake by Sylvia Weinstock Cakes, Ltd.
Florist: LMD Floral Events Interiors
Location: Private home
Calligraphy: Deborah Delaney

CHAPTER 5
All photographs by Shawn Connell, Christian Oth Studios, except pages 127, 132, 135, and 146, which are by Philippe Cheng
Cake by April Reed Cake Design

Florist: Glorimundi
Location: New York Public Library
Paper product: Russell Sloane
Calligraphy: Marian Rodenhizer

CHAPTER 6
Photographs by Christian Oth
Florist: Glorimundi
Location: Four Seasons Hotel, New York

CHAPTER 7
Photographs by Christian Oth
Cake by Margaret Braun
Invitation and menu cards: Russell Sloane
Caterer: Creative Edge Parties
Florist: LMD Floral Events Interiors
Location: West Side Loft
Calligraphy: Marian Rodenhizer

CHAPTER 8
Photographs by Jeremy Saladyga, Gruber Photographers New York
Cake by Sylvia Weinstock Cakes, Ltd.
Paper/card for Sunday breakfast: Russell Sloane
Florist: LMD Floral Events Interiors
Location: The Prince George Ballroom
Caterer: Sonnier & Castle Catering

CHAPTER 9
Photographs by Meredith Davenport, Christian Oth Photography
Paper products: Russell Sloane
Florist: Ariella Chezar
Location: Private home
Calligraphy: Michael Sull, The Lettering Design Group